C000269991

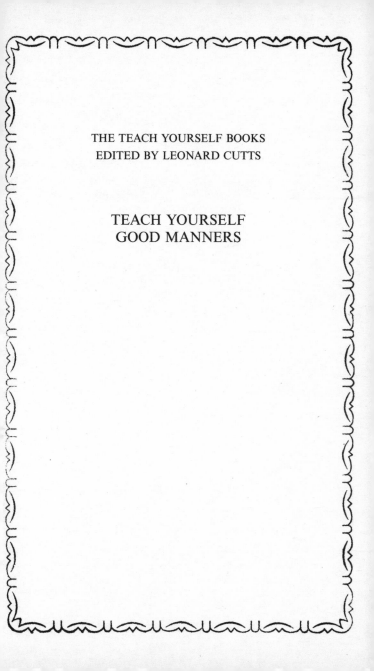

THE TEACH YOURSELF BOOKS
EDITED BY LEONARD CUTTS

TEACH YOURSELF
GOOD MANNERS

In the same series

———

Teach Yourself Bird Watching
Teach Yourself Cycling
Teach Yourself to Fly
Teach Yourself to Live

Teach®
Yourself

TEACH YOURSELF

GOOD
MANNERS

By
W. S. NORMAN

*Sketches by
Gordon Stowell*

First published in Great Britain in 1958.

This edition published in Great Britain in 2017 by John Murray Learning,
an imprint of Hodder & Stoughton. An Hachette UK company.

Previously published as *Teach Yourself Etiquette and Good Manners*

British Library Cataloguing in Publication Data: a catalogue
record for this title is available from the British Library.

Hardback: 978 1 473 66426 5
eBook: 978 1 473 66424 1

1

Cover image © Trinity Mirror / Mirrorpix / Alamy Stock Photo
Printed and bound in Great Britain by CPI Group (UK) Ltd., Croydon, CR0 4YY.

John Murray Learning policy is to use papers that are natural, renewable
and recyclable products and made from wood grown in sustainable forests.
The logging and manufacturing processes are expected to conform to
the environmental regulations of the country of origin.

Carmelite House
50 Victoria Embankment
London EC4Y 0DZ
www.hodder.co.uk

Also available
in ebook

CONTENTS

Introduction

Chapter I

Formal Communications to Royalty and
Nobility — The Superscription — The Beginning
— The Closing Words — Orders and Decorations
— What the Initials Stand for — Precedence of
Orders of Knighthood — The Privy Council —
Specimen Formal Notices — Courtesy Titles —
Forms of Address for Clergy, Judges, Mayors —
Beginning and Ending of Formal Communications
to them — Esquire — How and When to use it
— Omitted on Visiting Cards — Specimen Letters
to People of Title — A Communication Written
in the Third Person — Precedence in Great Britain.

Chapter II

In Letters — To Acquaintances and to Friends —
Specimen Letters by Way of Illustration — Spoken
Forms of Address — Speaking to or of Royalty and
Titled Persons — How *Not* to do it — Common
Errors — Unnecessary Repetition of Names —
Introductions: of one Individual to Another —
Useful Hints — Shaking Hands — Beginning a
Conversation — Introductions: of one Person to
a Group.

Chapter III

Chapter IV

Chapter V

CONTENTS

Chapter VI

TRAVEL 98

Staying at Hotels — Signing the Register — Behaviour in Hotels — Behaviour towards Fellowguests — Complaints — Visiting a Friend in a Hotel — Tipping in Hotels — Travelling Abroad — The Importance of Good Behaviour — National Customs — Presenting Letters of Introduction — Writing Letters of Introduction — The Wording — Specimen Letters of Introduction — Newcomers to a Place.

Chapter VII

GETTING ENGAGED . . . 112

Parental Influence — Consideration for Parents — Breaking the News — Announcing the Engagement — Forms of Announcement — The Engagement Ring — Length of the Engagement — Breaking Off an Engagement — Announcement of the Date of a Wedding — Choosing Wedding Presents — Acknowledging Wedding Presents.

Chapter VIII

GETTING MARRIED . . . 123

Choosing the Church — Date and Time of the Wedding — Publishing the Banns — The Officiating Clergy — Music at the Service — The Form of Service — Wedding Invitations — Sending Wedding Presents — Acknowledging a Wedding Invitation — Responsibility for Wedding Arrangements — Responsibilities of the Parents of the Bride — Expenses of the Bridegroom — The Bridesmaids — The Best Man — Rehearsals — The Ushers — Photographers — Arriving at the Church — The Wedding Ceremony — In the Vestry — Leaving the Church — Outside the Church — The Reception — Employing a Caterer — A Reception at a Private House — Receiving the Guests — Re-

INTRODUCTION

Why Bother about Etiquette?

A castaway on a desert island can behave as he likes because he has no one to consider except himself. But when Robinson Crusoe discovered footprints in the sand and became aware of the presence of Man Friday he could no longer act precisely as before. He had perforce

to take into account the existence of a companion and reckon with the possible effect of his behaviour and actions upon a second person. Two people thus suddenly brought face to face cannot ignore each other indefinitely. Either one must overcome the other or they must arrive, in the modern phrase, at some form of peaceful co-existence.

9

In the latter event they have first to convince each other of their friendly intentions. When an explorer comes upon a tribe of primitive people whose language he does not know, he will nod and smile, make friendly gestures and perhaps distribute small gifts. If these overtures are successful the tribesmen will take him to their village and bring him food and drink. Moreover the arrival of a distinguished visitor is something out of the ordinary: it is an event, an occasion. So, in response to an instinctive feeling that their guest should be treated as well as possible, something better than the ordinary fare will be provided, and the meal followed by singing and dancing. Politeness leads to hospitality, and the hospitality itself is carried out with a certain amount of ceremony, because it seems fitting. The host wishes to make his guest feel at home, the guest to show appreciation of the kindness he has received. So today if we have friends to dinner we give them as good a meal as we can—and are careful not to use that cracked soup-plate. The guest is at pains to show himself pleasant and entertaining, and will later, perhaps, write to thank us for an agreeable evening.

Questions of good behaviour and consideration for others arise whether round the tribal cooking-pot or the dinner table. Presumably they have arisen in one form or another since social life began, because social life is impossible if each person thinks only of himself. One suspects, indeed, that when a pre-historic man invited another to partake of a portion of pterodactyl steak (or even of a tender mutual neighbour) his guest would be expected to deposit his club tactfully at the cave-mouth (as we leave our umbrellas in the hall). The action would not have been meaningless, for it was evidence of good faith and pacific intention. It was, in short, a form of etiquette.

Sometimes a social usage is established for historical reasons. For instance, it is at least arguable that we use the right hand for shaking hands because in olden days when men wore swords, if each grasped the other's right hand, neither could draw upon the other. To hold

out the right hand was therefore a gesture of friendly intention. Sometimes a social usage is established simply for convenience. In this country, for example, to the confusion of other Europeans, except, at the moment, the Swedes, we drive on the left-hand side of the road. There is no merit in choosing the left rather than the right, but for the convenience of everybody a choice must be made and it so happened that, being sundered from the Continent by water, we made our choice without considering the views of other Europeans. Had we all chosen alike, car-manufacturers would have been better pleased. But unless some ruling had been made, the congestion on our roads would be even greater than it is today. If men are to live together in a community they must, as a measure of common sense and in the interest of the comfort and convenience of all, accept a certain number of rules and conventions. In a highly developed and complex society such general agreement is more than ever necessary. Chaos may result when four people play bridge according to widely different conventions. The same is true of social life.

The processes of birth and death are mysterious, the possibility of personal immortality a matter of faith or conjecture rather than of proof. It is natural therefore that from early times men should have attached importance to occasions marking the beginning and ending of life, to marriage, which heralds the coming of a new generation, or to an enthronement which inaugurates a new era. Each of these occasions therefore has led to the establishment by tribes and nations of rites and ceremonies of one kind and another, each being carried out in the manner that seemed most appropriate, and therefore entailing the observance of rules and customs. Hence both the elaborate ceremonial of a coronation in Westminster Abbey and the more simple procedure of a wedding in a village church.

There have been times when etiquette has been carried to absurd lengths, notably, for instance, at the Court of Louis XIV who varied his way of taking off his hat according to the social rank of the person whose salutation he was acknowledging. But etiquette, when not taken to excess, does not consist of a complicated and artificial code of rules calculated to trap the unwary or the inexperienced. It has little to do with snobbery or affectation. It is designed rather to make functions, whether informal or official, easier and more enjoyable alike for those who arrange and for those who attend them. It is based partly on recognised practice, sometimes hallowed by tradition, more often developed by experience, thanks to which social life can be led pleasurably because the procedure follows recognised lines and it is easy for people to know what to do. Secondly, it is based on good manners, and the essence of good manners is consideration for other people.

It might, of course, be argued that if a person has a kind heart and a friendly disposition, any ignorance on his part of social procedure is unimportant, because people will like him for himself. Up to a point that is quite true. For all that, however kind his heart or gentle his disposition, should we allow him full credit for these admirable qualities if—let us exaggerate—he came to lunch and blew his nose on the corner of the table-cloth? Even if he were not embarrassed, other people would be made uncomfortable. He would offend in two respects: by the coarseness of his own manners and in his lack of consideration for the feelings of others.

Again, when we meet people for the first time, our opinion of them is largely determined by the way in which they behave. We have, at that stage at least, no other means of judging. We may have been led to suppose that someone has a heart of gold, but we should find this hard to believe if he yawned ostentatiously in our faces while we were talking to him. Moreover, his lack of consideration entitles us to doubt the excellence of his character. Etiquette, let us repeat, does not consist only in observing certain rules of procedure. It does involve this, for the better conduct of social life and for ease and dignity of social intercourse. But it involves being pleasant rather than unpleasant, being polite to subordinates as well as to equals or superiors. It means showing concern for the comfort and convenience of others. To do this successfully calls both for good manners and for some knowledge of how to play one's own part, whether as host or guest, as principal or minor actor in the varied scenes of social life.

The Edwardian 'At Home', paying afternoon calls, leaving cards on people, having adequate domestic help —all these have virtually vanished from the contemporary scene, and little or nothing is said about them in this book. But at one time or another, we may have to write to a person of title, we stay in hotels, we entertain our friends at home or at restaurants. The majority of us were christened, many of us become engaged, get married and have children. All of us one day will die. It is with arrangements for such occasions and with the behaviour of people who organise or take part in them that this book is concerned.

CHAPTER I

FORMS OF ADDRESS

Formal Communications to Royalty and Nobility

Either in a private capacity or possibly as, say, Honorary Secretary of a Club or Society, any one of us may have occasion to write a letter, an invitation or some formal communication to people of title, serving officers, professional men and women, clergymen and others. For this we need to know the correct method of address. Within the compass of a small book it is not possible to deal with all the instances that may arise, but the following table, without being exhaustive, should be of use. It shows the style of address as it would appear on an envelope and as it would normally be repeated at the top left or bottom left corner of the letter contained in it. We may term this the superscription. The table shows also the opening and closing words which would be used in a *formal* communication:—

Person addressed	Superscription	Opening words	Closing words
1. The Sovereign	To the Queen's most Excellent Majesty.	Madam.	I remain, with profound veneration, Your Majesty's most faithful Servant.
2. A Royal Duke	To His Royal Highness the Duke of —	Sir	I remain, Sir, Your Royal Highness's most humble and obedient Servant.

3. A Duke	To His Grace the Duke of —	My Lord Duke	I remain, my Lord Duke, Your Grace's most obedient Servant.
4. A Duchess	To Her Grace the Duchess of —	Madam	I remain, Madam, Your Grace's most obedient Servant.
5. A Marquess *or* Marquis	To the Most Honourable the Marquess of —	My Lord Marquess	I remain, my Lord Marquess, Your Lordship's most obedient Servant.
6. An Earl	To the Right Honourable the Earl of —	My Lord	I remain, my Lord, Your Lordship's obedient Servant.
A Viscount	To the Right Honourable the Lord Viscount —	My Lord	I remain, my Lord, Your Lordship's obedient servant.
A Baron	To the Right Honourable the Lord —	My Lord	I remain, my Lord, Your Lordship's obedient servant.
7. Countess	The Right Honourable the Countess of —	Madam	I remain, Madam, Your Ladyship's most obedient Servant.
Viscountess	The Right Honourable the Viscountess —	Madam	I remain, Madam, Your Ladyship's most obedient Servant.
Lady (Baroness)	The Right Honourable the Lady —	Madam	I remain, Madam, Your Ladyship's most obedient Servant.
8. Baronet	Sir Thomas Penhaligon, Bart.	Sir	I remain, Sir, your most obedient Servant.
Knight	Sir Thomas Penhaligon	Sir	I remain, Sir, your most obedient Servant.

| 9. Wife of Baronet | Lady Cirencester | Madam | I remain, Madam, your most obedient Servant. |
| Wife of Knight | Lady Cirencester | Madam | I remain, Madam, your most obedient Servant. |

Of the above, Royal Dukes, Dukes, Marquesses, Earls, Viscounts and Barons are members of the Peerage and (failing some problematical future revision) have the hereditary right to sit in the House of Lords. By no means all of them do so with any frequency, nor, in fact, would there be room for them if they did. Baronets and Knights are not members of the Peerage. On the death of a Baronet the title passes to his heir, but a Knight's title lapses when he dies.

Orders and Decorations

If some distinguished person has consented, for example, to preside or speak at some meeting or to be the guest of honour at a dinner, it is proper that any notice or leaflet announcing the event should include not only his name and rank, but the initials of at least the more important honours which have been awarded to him. For a member of the Royal Family such additions would not be required, but otherwise they should be put in. But in what order?

Initials of Orders—Precedence.—As the Garter is the most ancient Order of Chivalry, the initials K.G. should obviously come first, but the membership of the Order, like that of the Thistle (K.T.) and of St. Patrick (K.P.) is small, so that this point will seldom arise. We are left therefore with the Six Orders of English Knighthood, namely:—

(i) the Bath, (ii) the Star of India, (iii) St. Michael and St. George, (iv) the Indian Empire, (v) the Royal Victorian Order, and (vi) the British Empire.

The above is the correct order of precedence,[1] so that if a man holds the highest rank in two of them, being, let us say, a Knight Grand Cross of the Order of the Bath and also of the Royal Victorian Order, the order of initials after his name would be:— G.C.B., G.C.V.O. However, should a man be a G.C.V.O. and a Knight Commander (but not a Knight Grand Cross) of the Bath, it would then be correct to put G.C.V.O. first and K.C.B. second, because although the Bath takes precedence of the Royal Victorian Order, the higher rank in the second would take precedence over a lower rank in the first. Similarly a Knight Commander of the Order of the British Empire (K.B.E.)[2] would take precedence over a Companion of the Bath (C.B.) because of the difference in rank in the respective Orders. In the same way a Companion of the Distinguished Service Order (D.S.O.) who was also an Officer of the British Empire (O.B.E.) would have his distinctions listed in that order because, although the initials do not indicate it, he is a "companion" of the former and only an "officer" of the latter. The Victoria Cross, by the way, is worn before all other decorations, and the George Cross before all others except the Victoria Cross.

[1] There are also Knights Bachelor, that is those who are Knights, but not members of any of the above Orders—e.g. the actor Sir Henry Irving and subsequent members of that profession who have been knighted. In the order of precedence they come after members of the six Orders.

[2] For women the equivalent of K.B.E. is D.B.E. (Dame Commander), but the initials G.B.E., C.B.E., O.B.E. and M.B.E. are applicable to both men and women.

The Privy Council

The Privy Council is a very ancient body. Members of the Cabinet are always Privy Councillors. In practice they constitute the majority of the active Council, but former members of it still retain the right to the letters P.C. after their names, so that the total number is likely to be about three hundred. Every Privy Councillor has by custom the right to be described as "the Right Honourable." In the order of precedence a Privy Councillor in virtue of his office comes before a G.C.B. It is worth bearing in mind also that a Member of the Order of Merit (O.M.),[1] though membership carries no title with it, ranks immediately after a G.C.B. and before, for example, a G.C.M.G. (Knight Grand Cross of St. Michael and St. George). A Companion of Honour (C.H.)[2] would come after a G.B.E., but before a Knight Commander of any of the six orders of knighthood that were listed above. Finally, to round off this summary with a generalisation, it may be said that lawyers who have taken silk and are therefore Queen's Counsel (Q.C.) and graduates of Universities (M.A., Ll.B., etc.) would normally put these initials after any others to which they may be entitled. For a Member of Parliament the letters M.P. would be placed last of all.

The following examples will serve to illustrate the observations made in the foregoing paragraphs:—

1. Admiral Sir Sefton Saltair, K.B.E., C.B., D.S.O., R.N.
2. Professor Sir Edward Lancet, M.V.O., F.R.C.P., F.R.S.

---

[1] Apart from foreign honorary members (e.g. D. D. Eisenhower 1945) the Order is limited to 24 members, military or civil.

[2] The Companions of Honour are limited to 65 in number. The Order, like the Order of Merit, is open to women as well as to men.

3. The Right Hon. William Crossbench, P.C., M.C., Q.C., M.P.
4. The Most Hon. the Marquess of Uttoxeter, K.G.
5. Air-Commodore Sir David Javelin, K.B.E., C.B., M.C., F.R.S.
6. Matthew Small, Esq., C.H., M.P.
7. Dame Miriam Spencer, D.B.E.

Special Formal Notices

Such are the forms likely to be used in printed or written documents of a *formal or official* kind. Here are some examples:—

1.   East Surrey Apiarists' Society

The Annual General Meeting of the Society will be held in the Lower Room of the Pavilion, Oldchester on Saturday, 7 May, 19— at 5.0 p.m.

The Agenda will be circulated in advance. The Chair will be taken by the President of the Society, Dr. A. F. Masters, Sc.D., F.R.S., J.P.

R.S.V.P. to H. Pollen (Hon. Sec.) The Skips,
Hiving.

2.   King George II School, Cranwich

The Chairman and the Board of Governors request the honour of the company of...............
on the occasion of the opening of the new Library
by
Air Chief Marshal the Earl of Malton,
G.C.B., G.B.E., D.F.C.
(President of the Old Georgian Association)
at 3.0 p.m. on Wednesday, 8 July, 19—

It will greatly facilitate arrangements if you will kindly send your reply to the Bursar, not later than 20 June.

3. Old Georgians Cricket Club

Annual Dinner

at

The Croesus Restaurant, Park Lane, W.1.

on

Saturday, 6 July, 19—, at 7.45 p.m. (for 8.0 p.m.)

The Toast of the Club will be proposed by the President, General Sir Arnold Conybeare, Bt., K.C.B., C.I.E., M.C.

Tickets (price 30/– each, exclusive of wines) from the Hon. Sec. (S. C. Rounge), 54 Carey St., London, S.W.3.

Dress: Dinner Jacket.

Courtesy Titles

A peer is succeeded on his death by his heir, usually no doubt, his eldest son, who then assumes his late father's title. But what title, if any, did this heir bear in his father's lifetime?

Essentially (though it admits of complications) the system is simple and rests upon the fact that no commoner (i.e. untitled person), however great the services he may render to the State, will be created a Duke without having first held some lower rank in the Peerage. It must, indeed, be extremely rare for the transition from commoner to duke to be made in the span of a single lifetime: usually this process would extend over two or more generations. But the attainment of a higher rank in the peerage does not mean that the person so honoured relinquishes the lower from which he has been promoted.

Any such earlier title is retained in the family, so that the eldest son of a Duke or of a Marquess takes by courtesy his father's second title (which is likely to be Earl or Viscount) and holds it until his father's death. The remaining sons of a Duke or Marquess and all the daughters are styled by courtesy (The) Lord (Lady)

followed by their Christian name and family surname: e.g. (The) Lord Charles Cotswold, (The) Lady Helen Grampian.

In the same way the eldest son of an Earl bears his father's second title (perhaps that of Viscount) but his younger brothers are styled the Honourable,[1] followed by the Christian name and surname, e.g. the Hon. Francis Mendip. His sisters (like the daughters of Dukes and Marquesses) put Lady before their Christian Name and surname: e.g. (The) Lady Mary Southdown.

The eldest sons of Viscounts and Barons enjoy no such distinctive title for they, their brothers and their sisters are all treated alike, the style being the Hon. Robert (Jane) Quantock.

Thus the Hon. George Piltdown might be the second son of an Earl or the eldest (or youngest) son of a Viscount or of a Baron. As already mentioned Baronets and Knights are not Peers. The heirs of the former have

[1] Not to be confused with the Right Honourable applied to a member of the Privy Council.

no title until they succeed to the baronetcy, while a Knight's title lapses at his death.

Forms of Address:—

Clergy, Judges and others. Here again it will be useful to set out in tabular form the superscription, beginning and ending of formal or official communications addressed to clergy, judicial officers and others with whom so far we have not been concerned:—

Person addressed	Superscription	Beginning	Ending
1. Archbishops	His Grace the Lord Archbishop of Canterbury (York)	My Lord Archbishop	I remain, my Lord Archbishop, Your Grace's most obedient Servant.
2. A Bishop[1]	The Right Rev. the Lord Bishop of —	My Lord My Lord Bishop	Your Lordship's most obedient Servant.
3. A Dean	The Very Rev. the Dean of —	Reverend Sir Dear Mr. Dean	I remain, Reverend Sir, Your most obedient Servant.
4. An Archdeacon	The Venerable the Archdeacon of —	Reverend Sir Dear Mr. Archdeacon	I remain, Reverend Sir, Your most obedient Servant.
5. A Canon	The Rev. Canon S. Dodds	Dear Sir Reverend Sir	I have the honour to be, Sir, yours faithfully.
6. A Rector[2]	The Rev. A. H. Drew	Reverend Sir Dear Sir	I have the honour to be, Sir, yours faithfully.

[1] The two Archbishops, the Bishops of London, Durham and Winchester and 21 others (chosen by the date of their appointment) have seats in the House of Lords.

[2] It is wrong to say or to write: "The Rev(erend) Robinson. In writing or, for example, in announcing a speaker (or preacher), the correct form is The Rev. Stephen (*or* The Rev. S.) Robinson. Informally "Mr. Robinson" or "the Rector" is correct: but with "the Rev." the Christian name or initials must be inserted before the surname.

A Vicar	The Rev. A. H. Drew	Reverend Sir Dear Sir	I have the honour to be, Sir, yours faithfully.
A Curate	The Rev. A. H. Drew	Reverend Sir Dear Sir	I have the honour to be, Sir, yours faithfully.
A Presbyterian Minister	The Rev. A. H. Drew	Reverend Sir Dear Sir	I have the honour to be, Sir, yours faithfully.
A Wesleyan (Baptist) Minister	The Rev. A. H. Drew	Reverend Sir Dear Sir	I have the honour to be, Sir, yours faithfully.
7. A Cardinal	His Eminence Bernard, Cardinal Griffin	Your Eminence	Your most obedient Servant.
	His Eminence the Cardinal Archbishop of —	Your Eminence	Your most obedient Servant.
8. A Lord of Appeal in Ordinary	The Right Honourable Lord —	My Lord	I have the honour to be, with great respect, your Lordship's most obedient Servant.
A Judge of the High Court	The Hon. Mr. Justice Quick	Sir	I have the honour to be, Sir, your obedient Servant.
	or His Honour Sir J. Quick, Kt.	My Lord (when on the Bench)	I have the honour to be, Sir, your obedient Servant.
A County Court Judge	His Honour Judge Clerendon	Sir Your Honour (when on the Bench)	I beg to remain, Sir, your obedient Servant.
A Justice of the Peace	The Right Worshipful—J.P. or James Short, Esq., J.P.	Sir Your Worship (when on the Bench)	Yours faithfully.
9. A Lord Mayor	The Right Hon. the Lord Mayor of —	My Lord My Lord Mayor	Your Lordship's most obedient Servant.

A Mayor (City)	The Right Worshipful the Mayor of —	Sir	I remain, Sir, yours faithfully.

Your Worship (on the Bench)

A Mayor (Borough)	The Worshipful the Mayor of —	Sir Mr. Mayor[1] (at a meeting)	I remain, Sir, yours faithfully.

Esquire

Strictly, the title of Esquire belongs only to certain classes of people, such as younger sons of peers, barristers-at-law, mayors during their term of office, and the eldest sons of baronets and knights. In practice the term became of much wider application and was extended by custom to professional and business men, though not to retail tradesmen or artisans. As against this more liberal usage a tendency in the opposite direction has developed since about 1945 by which even those who according to the strictest interpretation would be entitled to the description of Esquire are denied it and addressed along with everyone else as plain Mr. It is true that under the former usage many people had Esq. put after their names when they had no legal right to it. But if one must err it is surely better to do so on the side of politeness and civility. The wisest course therefore when addressing an envelope is to go beyond the former custom and to be more, rather than less, lavish in using the abbreviation Esq. There are, however, one or two points to bear in mind:—

[1] When the Mayor is a lady it is still usual to address her as "Mr. Mayor", though when a lady takes a Chair at a meeting, she is likely to be addressed as "Madam Chairman", but the usage varies, e.g. "Mr. Mayor, you also are a mother."

1. It is proper, when writing, to address a Lieutenant or a Sub-Lieutenant of the Royal Navy or a 1st Lieutenant or a 2nd Lieutenant of the Army as Esquire, e.g.:—

(*a*) J. McBride, Esq., R.N.

(*b*) John Turner, Esq., M.C.

But,

(*c*) Captain J. L. Firth, R.N. (Rtd.), and

(*d*) Major Alan Forbes, R.A.S.C.

2. Save for the above exceptions, Esquire is essentially a civilian term. It cannot be used of clergy. It is used in writing *instead* of Mr. and not as well as it. Similarly, it is wrong to write Dr. J. Smith, Esq.; Dr. J. Smith is correct, but J. Smith, Esq. would be wrong, because Esq. is a substitute only for Mr., and the person concerned has certain professional qualifications which entitle him to be known as Dr., in much the same way as an officer reaches the rank of and is therefore entitled to be described as Major (not Mr.) So-and-So.

3. Although nowadays almost any adult male may on occasion be addressed as Esquire (or Esq. for short), the term in its original sense meant that the person concerned, either by birth or position, was of more social consequence than most other people. It follows therefore that (although this may smack of mock-modesty) it would be pretentious to describe oneself as Esquire. Thus when enclosing with a letter a stamped envelope for reply addressed to oneself it is better either voluntarily to step down a peg and put Mr. S. Y. Jones on this envelope or else to put simply S. Y. Jones, leaving your correspondent (if he is tactful) to insert Esq. after your name, or (if he wants to snub you) to put Mr. before it.

Omitted on Visiting Cards

In this connection it is worth remarking that, for the same reason, it is incorrect to put Esq. after one's name on a visiting card, which should read Mr. S. Y. Jones or Mr. Samuel Jones. One need hardly add that, because it would be ostentatious and boastful, no mention of orders and decorations should be made on a visiting card. It is,

however, perfectly correct for anybody of the rank of knight and upwards to put his title before his name on his card, since this merely replaces the Mr. of the ordinary commoner.

Specimen Letters

The correct style of address in strictly formal communications has already been shown, but nothing has yet been said of the content of such communications. As this will obviously vary according to the subject matter, no rules can be laid down, but some sample letters of this formal kind may be of some use as a guide, so here follow a few examples:—

1.

To His Grace   The Girdlestone Art Gallery,
the Duke of Uttoxeter, K.G. Constable Square,
Rollesbury Hall,   Marston.
Midshire.   4th July, 19—

My Lord Duke,
  It may already have come to Your Grace's notice that, as recently made known in the press, the Fine Arts Committee of the County intend next spring to hold at the Girdlestone Art Gallery an Exhibition of French 18th Century paintings.

  Since it is hoped to make this Exhibition as representative as possible, I have been instructed by the Committee to enquire whether Your Grace would generously permit us to show for the period of the Exhibition (1st Feb.—15th March) a few of the very fine pictures in your own collection, and, in particular, the portrait of Her Grace the 5th Duchess of Uttoxeter by Boucher.

  I need hardly emphasize how deeply the Chairman and the Committee would appreciate Your Grace's kindness should you feel able to accede to this request, and how greatly the loan of these pictures would add to the artistic value and to the success of the Exhibition.

       I remain, My Lord Duke,
       Your Grace's most obedient Servant,
         C. Adge (Curator).

2.

Lady Tulse,[1]   The Rectory,
Beckenham Lodge,   Little Warmington,
Southgate.   Surrey.
                                           2nd April, 19—

Madam,

For many years you have, I know, taken an active interest in many charitable enterprises and good causes, particularly in the work of missionary organisations overseas. Despite the many calls already made, no doubt, upon your time, I am therefore venturing to ask whether you would very kindly consent to open the Annual Bazaar to be held on the afternoon of Wednesday, 12th June, at the Guildhall, Warmington, in aid of the Church of England Polynesian Missionary Society. This Society is doing admirable work and the Dean of Warmington, who will preside, is most anxious, as indeed we all are, that its activities should not only be maintained, but extended.

If, as I greatly hope, you can find time to help the Society in this way, I will send you further information or, if you would prefer it, call to discuss arrangements at any time convenient to yourself.

I remain, Madam,

Your most obedient Servant,

J. N. Apsley (Organising Secretary).

[1] The absence of any Christian name or initial indicates that this lady is the wife of a baronet or knight.

3.   (In the third person).   Half Seas,
     T. Burke, Esq.   Over,
     The Oaks,   Cambs.
     Over.   1st August, 19—

Admiral Deepwater presents his compliments to
Mr. Burke and wishes to point out to him that owing
to his continued failure to repair the fence dividing
the two properties Mr. Burke's cows have again
strayed into the Admiral's kitchen garden and have
now entirely destroyed the vegetable marrows which
it had been his intention to enter in the forthcoming
Fruit and Vegetable Show. The Admiral has made
repeated representations to Mr. Burke on this
matter in the past. In view of this latest outrage he
now informs him that, unless repairs to the fence
are undertaken forthwith, he will institute legal
proceedings.

Precedence in Great Britain

In the section of this chapter concerned with orders
and decorations it was stated that if some distinguished
person was both a G.C.B. and a G.B.E. the initials
would appear in that order after his name, since the
Order of the Bath takes precedence over the Order of
the British Empire. It follows that in a ceremonial
procession a holder of the former would come before
a holder of the latter.

To avoid possible error it should be said that, notwith-
standing the point just made, it is quite possible that in
such a ceremonial procession a G.B.E. would in fact
occupy a more prominent position than a G.C.B. The
reason is that his precise place might be determined, not

by his membership of a given Order, but by his rank in the peerage or his holding of a particular office. For example, the Archbishop of Canterbury, in virtue of his office, takes precedence over everyone except the Sovereign and the Royal Dukes, with the Prime Minister, who is now almost always a commoner, following immediately behind him. In the same way a Duke takes pride of place over a Marquess (regardless of what letters either may be entitled to put after his name) simply because a dukedom is a higher rank in the peerage than a marquisate.

The whole order of precedence in Great Britain from the Sovereign to the younger son of a Knight is fully given in works such as Whitaker's Almanack, to which, when the need arises, reference can readily be made. If no such order were laid down the greatest confusion and uncertainty would prevail, as well as indignation on the part of some who found themselves ousted by more thrustful persons from their rightful place. It is bad enough when three or four people hover uncertainly in front of a door wondering which of them should pass through it first. On a great ceremonial occasion the result would be chaotic were it not for well-established usage. The court of Macbeth was hardly a model one. But it is clear that etiquette was observed there, because in a sudden emergency Lady Macbeth found it necessary to urge the courtiers not to stand upon the order of their going, but to go at once. The reason, it will be remembered, was that the newly murdered Banquo had walked into the banqueting hall, and the appearance of this ghostly gatecrasher had scared Macbeth out of his wits. But it was only in this exceptional circumstance that etiquette was disregarded.

The reader who has persevered so far, may perhaps be thinking that up to this point this book has been concerned almost exclusively with the aristocracy. "I

am not in the habit of writing to peers" he may say, "nor does it ordinarily matter to me whether a baronet or a viscount should take the place of honour." But that is precisely the point. If we ordinarily moved in such circles we should know these things. It is because they come our way but rarely that we need to be informed about them, so that we can deal with the occasional situation when or if it does arise. But we can turn now from the ceremonious to the somewhat less formal.

CHAPTER II

FORMS OF ADDRESS
(CONTINUED)

In Letters

In the first chapter it was assumed throughout that the person writing either had no acquaintance at all with his correspondent or that, if he had, the communication was of a strictly formal or official nature. In the present chapter therefore we need not consider further correspondence of that kind. Nor need we trouble ourselves with the forms of address to be used in private correspondence between two old and intimate friends.

Writing to Acquaintances and Friends

If in your youth you were in the habit of throwing paper darts artfully dipped in ink at a schoolfellow and have in subsequent years kept in close touch with him, the fact that he later became a bishop or a cabinet minister, whereas you have attained no such eminence, need not affect the terms in which you write to him. In a personal letter you can continue to address him by his Christian name (or even his nickname), however dignified and formal the superscription on the envelope may be. Such letters present no difficulty.

But there is an intermediate stage between formality on the one hand and intimacy on the other. If one writes officially to a Duke we shall need, as we have seen, to begin: "My Lord Duke," whereas in the event,

33

admittedly unlikely, of our having shared a desk with him in the Lower Fourth, we might in a personal letter call him "Dear Bill." Similarly in a letter to, say, a clerk or a policeman, the alternatives range from 'Sir'

or 'Dear Sir' to 'My dear Fred'. We have therefore to consider the form of address to be adopted in writing to people, whether titled or not, whom we know slightly or fairly well. The suggested openings may conveniently be set out in the form of a table.

Person addressed	From an acquaintance	From a friend
A Duke	My dear Duke of —	Dear Duke
A Duchess	My Dear Duchess of —	Dear Duchess
A Marquess	Dear Lord (Southport)	My dear Lord (Southport)
A Marquess	,, ,,	,, ,, ,,
An Earl	,, ,,	,, ,, ,,
A Viscount	,, ,,	,, ,, ,,
A Baron	,, ,,	,, ,, ,,
A Marchioness	Dear Lady (Southport)	My dear Lady (Southport)
A Countess	,, ,,	,, ,, ,,
A Viscountess	,, ,,	,, ,, ,,
A Baroness	,, ,,	,, ,, ,,

A Baronet	Dear Sir Henry	My dear Sir Henry[1]
A Knight	,, ,, ,,	,, ,, ,, ,,
Wife of Baronet	Dear Lady Cowfold	My dear Lady Cowfold[2]
Wife of Knight	,, ,, ,,	,, ,, ,, ,,
A Bishop	Dear Bishop	(My) dear Bishop.
A Canon	Dear Canon Jones	Dear Canon Jones
	Dear Canon	
A Vicar	Dear Mr. Jones	Dear Mr. Jones
		Dear Vicar

Specimen Letters

The above examples must serve, though it is impossible to lay down hard and fast rules about friendly as opposed to formal correspondence, since much depends on the degree of friendship and on the circumstances. For instance, one person might write to a Colonel as "Dear Colonel Jones", whereas another knowing him better might omit the 'Colonel' or put the Christian instead of the surname. Again, in writing to a clergyman the normal beginning would be "Dear Mr. Foster," but a church-warden might very well begin his letter with "My dear Vicar." Similarly endings would range from the "Yours very truly" of slight acquaintanceship to the "Yours ever" of intimacy, with a very wide intermediate stage covered by "Yours sincerely".

Here then, as samples, not as unvarying models, are three letters, each dealing with the same subject, but implying, in each case, a different degree of friendship.

[1] A man (but not a woman), might well put "Dear Barker," rather than "(My) dear Sir Henry," just as when writing to an untitled friend or acquaintance he might put "Dear Barker" (omitting the "Mr.").

[2] In this style of address there is nothing to differentiate between the wife of a Baronet or the wife of a Baron, but on the envelope the superscription would be in the former case 'Lady Cowfold' and in the latter 'The Lady Southport'. If, on the other hand, the lady is the daughter of, let us say, an Earl, or a Marquess, the envelope would be addressed to 'The Lady Mary Southport' (the Christian name is essential) and the letter itself could begin: "Dear Lady Mary Southport" or, more intimately, "Dear Lady Mary."

1.

The Viscountess Lavenham,   25, Portminster Square,
17, East Audley St.,   W.3.
London, S.W.1.   11th July, 19—

Dear Lady Lavenham,

When I had the pleasure of talking with you at
the Dersingham's last week, you mentioned Sartre's
new play, now running at the Thespian, and said
that you would like to read it. On making enquiries
I was confirmed in my belief that the text of the
play has not yet been published over here. As it
happens, I saw it in Paris last year and I find I still
have a copy of the French edition.

Nothing is more tiresome than having a book
foisted on one, but if you would really like to read
this play, I will gladly let you have my copy. In that
case perhaps you would allow me to bring it round
to you.

> I remain, Dear Lady Lavenham,
> Yours sincerely,
> Arthur Willoughby.

2.

Professor J. H. Tweed,   25, Palmerston St.,
The Haven,   Dorking.
Longwind,   25th October, 19—
Berks.

Dear Professor Tweed,

You will probably not remember me, but in my
undergraduate days now—alas!—a good many years
ago, I used to attend your lectures.

In last Sunday's *Standard* I chanced to see your

letter in which you stated that you were working
on a biography of Mendelssohn and enquired whether
any readers of that paper had in their possession any
letters or original material concerning him. It
occurred to me that I might be able to help you.

My grandfather, who was a keen amateur
musician, corresponded with Mendelssohn and, I
believe, met him several times. I am vague about the
details, as it all happened before my time, but I still
have a kind of scrap-book containing one or two
letters from Mendelssohn and a number of press
cuttings relating to performances of his works in
London. They are of no great interest to me, but in
the hope that they may be to you, I am sending the
book to you by registered post.

Yours very truly,
J. H. Huntley (St. Bede's 1928-31).

3.

Captain J. A. Dawkins,	The Beck,
c/o The Nomads' Club,	Peel,
S.W.3.	Isle of Man.
	2nd September, 19—

Dear Dawker,

At your urgent request I was misguided enough
to lend you my cherished copy of Dodge's *Fly Fish-
ing*, which has been my stand-by for years. I ought
to have known better. As if there aren't enough gaps
on my shelves already to remind me that it is fatal to
lend books to otherwise tolerably honest friends!
You've had it for at least six months and I haven't
the foggiest idea where you are. Probably bagging
the largest salmon in Norway, which you'd never be

able to do without my book. So send it back before I have the law on you!

My love to Muriel, and all the best to you, though you don't deserve it!

Yours ever,
Gordon.

Spoken Forms of Address

The radio has accustomed us to hearing such opening words as "Your Royal Highness, Your Grace, Your Excellencies, My Lords, Ladies and Gentlemen." It follows from this that in any speech made on an occasion when the Queen is present, it is necessary to say "Your Majesty" (because whoever else may be there, the speech will in the first instance be addressed to her) and also when speaking on the same occasion to refer to the Duke of Edinburgh as "His Royal Highness."

Should you, as an individual, have the honour of being presented to the Queen, it would be permissible to use the phrase "Your Majesty" in answer to the first remark or question that she might be graciously pleased to address to you, but in any further reply you should call her "Ma'am". This applies only when answering. Should you have the occasion to put a direct question to the Queen, it would always be correct to address her as "Your Majesty." Similarly you could address H.R.H. the Duke of Edinburgh as "Your Royal Highness," but when answering, you would call him "Sir". In the same way when replying to any observation addressed to you by a member of the Royal Family, you should use 'Sir' or 'Ma'am', whichever is appropriate.

It remains to add that if in the presence of one member of the Royal Family you have occasion to refer to another member of it, it would be wrong to speak of 'the Queen', 'the Duke of Edinburgh' or 'the Duchess of Gloucester'. The correct forms under these circumstances are, respectively, "Her Majesty", "His Royal Highness", and "Her Royal Highness."

In formal communications, as we have seen, it is correct to write to a member of the peerage as, let us say, 'The Most Hon. the Marquess of Todmorden' or 'The Right Hon. the Earl of Symington'. A friend writing to such people would omit from the super-scription 'The Most Hon'. and 'The Right Hon.' and would begin his letter with "Dear Lord Todmorden (Symington)" that is, assuming that he was not sufficiently intimate with him to use the Christian name or the surname by itself.

Members of the peerage meeting each other require no help from this or any other book to know how they should address one another. But we, as commoners, may need to know how in conversation we should speak to a person of title whom we may meet at some function or at a social gathering.

How Not to do it

In a certain radio programme listeners used to be invited to look out for "a deliberate mistake."

The following passage of dialogue between two imaginary people of title contains a number of errors. To spot them will not require much effort, but perhaps enough to divert the reader's attention from the deplorably banal quality of the conversation.

She: Do remind me, Viscount Withington. When was it you mentioned you had met the Honour-able Mr. Sugden?

He: At the Earl of Foxton's. He's a cousin of mine.

She: Who is? The Honourable?

He: No. The Earl. To be exact a connection, rather
           than a cousin. He married my second cousin,
           the Duke of Bristol's youngest daughter.

She: Oh! The Lady Joan Milverton?

He: Yes. That's the one.

(During this enthralling conversation, she has pressed
the bell. As this is fiction, not real life, a deferential
butler has appeared.)

She: My tyrant of a doctor won't let me touch a
           thing between meals, but I'm sure you'd like
           a drink. James will bring you anything you like.

He: Thank you. In that case, I'd like a dry sherry.

Butler: Very good, Your Grace.

It would be painful to continue. Let us look at some
of the mistakes.

1. *Viscount Withington.*—In talking to a Duke or a
Duchess (other than Royalty) it would be correct to
say, for example: "Do you remember, Duchess, that
when we last met, etc." This usage is not employed
when speaking to (or usually of) Marquesses, Earls,
Viscounts, Barons and their wives. An acquaintance
(i.e. someone not on more friendly terms) would normally
say simply: "Lord Withington (Lady Smythe)" no matter
to which of these four ranks in the peerage the person
addressed belonged.

2. *The Honourable Mr. Sugden.*—This is not used,
either in conversation, or even on a visiting card. A
speaker not knowing the person concerned would refer

to him as Mr. Sugden. A friend might say: "I used to know John Sugden (or Sugden) fairly well."

3. *At the Earl of Foxton's.*—The speaker here is supposed to be a relative or a connection of his. He would therefore say: "At the Foxton's," while an acquaintance might say: "At Lord Foxton's."

4. *The Honourable. The Earl.* See 2 and 3 above.

5. *The Duke of Bristol's* youngest daughter. A viscount, talking about a ducal relative, presumably known to both of them, would surely say simply: "Bristol's youngest daughter."

6. *The Lady Joan Milverton.*—This is the formal description. In speaking to or about the daughter of a Duke, a Marquess or an Earl, the 'The' would be dropped, leaving Lady Joan Milverton. A friend in conversation or in a letter would shorten it further to 'Lady Joan'.

7. *Your Grace.*—If the butler were addressing a Duke, this would be correct, but he is not. For a Marquess, Viscount, Earl or Baron, the proper form is "My Lord". In talking *about* such a person the butler would say "His Lordship."

The, or at least a, correct version of the passage would therefore run as follows:—

She: Do remind me, Lord Withington. When did you say you had met Mr. Sugden (or John Sugden)?

He: At the Foxton's. He's a cousin of mine.

She: Who is? Mr. Sugden?

He: No. Foxton. To be exact, a connection rather than a cousin. He married my second cousin, Bristol's youngest girl.

She: Oh! Lady Joan Milverton.

EGM—B*

He: Yes. That's the one.

(The butler enters)

She: My tyrant of a doctor won't let me touch a thing between meals, but I'm sure you'd like a drink. Just tell James what you'd like.

He: That's very kind of you. A dry sherry, I think.

Butler: Very good, my Lord.

Unnecessary Repetition of Names

Once greetings are over it is seldom necessary to mention again the names of the parties to a conversation. It is tiresome when someone consistently repeats, out of misguided politeness, the name of the person he is talking to. It may, of course, be necessary to mention it, when bringing a third party into the conversation: e.g. "As I was saying to Mrs. Brewster just before you arrived." Usually, however, names are mentioned in making introductions rather than in an ensuing conversation. Since introductions will obviously be made at the beginning of an acquaintanceship, it is important that they should be performed properly. Often they are not. This may make things awkward, especially for shy or nervous people, just when it is desirable that they should be put at ease. Let us therefore mention a few points to be borne in mind when making people known to one another.

Introductions.—*Of one individual to another, by means of a third person.*

If both are men, introduce the younger to the older, not the other way round.

If both are women, one being married and the other not, introduce the single one to the other.

If both are married or both single, introduce the younger to the older.

If one is a man and the other a woman, introduce the man to the woman, not vice-versa.[1]

Useful Hints

In making an introduction, don't mumble, but pronounce both names distinctly. Not everyone does this. Many Americans, when introduced, have a sensible habit of repeating the name of the person just made known to them, which gives the other the opportunity to correct it, if he has not heard it properly. (But if your name is a difficult one, resign yourself with a good grace to hearing it mispronounced rather than make the other person feel embarrassed at having got it wrong.) If the introducer has mumbled, it is better for one of the new acquaintances to say frankly to the other: "I'm sorry, I didn't catch your name?" This enables the other, who may be in like case, to give his name and, if need be, make the same remark. If you don't make sure in this way, you may have to ask on some later occasion, and it is much better to do this at a first rather than at a third meeting.

If two individuals are introduced each should shake the other's hand. This does not mean crush it, pulverise it, paw it, pump it up and down or retain it. The owner wants it back, quickly and intact. So take it lightly but firmly, looking at its owner while you do so, not at someone else, then let it go. Nothing is worse than

---

[1] But should a man be a member of the Royal family, a guest of honour at a function or otherwise distinguished, it would then be correct to introduce a woman to him, not him to the woman.

poking out a hesitant hand and then uncertainly with-drawing it. Be definite but brief. If the introduction takes place out of doors, a man, who is wearing a glove, should take it off. Indeed if he thinks an introduction likely he should take it off in advance, rather than

fumble with it while the other's hand is already stretched out. Shaking hands may be dispensed with if the hands of one or both are already full of parcels and the like. There are times when tact and common sense are more important than strict observance of a convention.

If a man is introduced to a lady who is sitting down, she should not get up. If, following the introduction, the pair begin to talk, the man, after a moment or two should say "May I sit down?" and do so.

Beginning a Conversation

When two people are introduced to each other, both should say "How do you do?" This does not call for an answer and is a purely conventional phrase. But it is a better one than "Pleased to meet you." (If, after this conventional greeting you really want to enquire after the other's health the words "How are you?" pave the way for an organ recital. But make it brief and reserve it, in any case, for an acquaintance or friend, not for someone you have only just met.)

It is not always easy to begin a conversation with someone to whom one has only just been introduced. An experienced introducer can do much to break the ice by hinting at a subject which might provide a starting point. Thus: "Mrs Huxtable, may I introduce Mr. Chalmers to you? He used to live in your part of the world." Or: "Miss Hankey, I don't believe you've met John Graham—Mr. Graham—Miss Hankey. Like you, he's very interested in the theatre."

Naturally, this cannot always be done. The host may not have a clue to their interests. He may merely mumble two names and then disappear, leaving them to manage as best they can.

If when you are walking with a friend, your companion sees someone whom he knows and you do not, you should move away a little, leaving it to your companion to call you over if he wants to introduce you. This applies even more if the friend is a lady. He would then normally ask her permission before introducing you.

Introductions.—*Of one person to a group.*

Here the same general principles would apply. Ideally the introducer should know the names of all concerned. He would then lead up the newcomer and say to the group: "This is James Thurston (possibly "Mr. Thurston") whom I want to introduce to you." Then, indicating each of the group in turn: "Mr. Thurston—Miss A, Mr. B, Mrs. C, Miss E. and Mr. F." Strictly, perhaps, he should introduce him to the ladies first, but this may be complicated, and it would be permissible to go by the order in which they happen to be standing.

If, as is liable to happen, the introducer momentarily forgets or does not in fact know the name of one of the group, it is up to that person (Guests have obligations as well as hosts) to come to the rescue by saying: "I'm Muriel Hay. How do you do?" or something of the sort.

In France the newcomer would shake hands all round. In this country, he need not, if to do so would mean a lot of moving about (as round a table, for instance). But he should say "How d'you do" and bow slightly to the owner of each name as it is uttered. If the host then goes on his way, one of the group should have the good manners to address some remark to the newcomer and draw him into the conversation.

Introductions of this kind, involving a group of people, may take place in a family circle. But they are more likely to occur at a party of some sort. When a party is given the people present will have been invited to it. In short before there is a party there must have been invitations. Let us now therefore consider the various forms that invitations usually take and the replies that should be sent to them.

CHAPTER III

INVITATIONS

To Formal Functions

In the first chapter we considered formal styles of address. It follows that when issuing an invitation to an official or formal function, the wording of the invitation would differ from that to be used when inviting a friend to lunch.

Among formal functions would be, let us say, a dinner or a reception given by a City Company, a Regiment, a College or University or by the Mayor and Corporation of a borough. Invitations to such a function would therefore be in the form of a printed or engraved card, with a space left blank on it, in which would be inserted in ink the name(s) of the individual(s) to which the particular card is to be sent. It would be the business of the organizer (e.g. secretary) to arrange for the printing of the cards and for sending out the complete invitations. Below are one or two examples of such invitation cards:—

City of Westchester

The Mayor and Corporation of Westchester

request the honour of the company of

....

at a Reception in the Mayor's Parlour

on Saturday, 5th December, at 9.0 p.m.

Evening Dress.   R.S.V.P.

The Town Clerk,

Westchester.

The Warden and Mastercraftsmen of the
Guild of Lacemakers
request the honour of the company of

....

at Dinner
in the Lacemakers' Hall, Threadneedle St.,
on Wednesday, 6th July at 7.45 p.m.

Decorations will be worn.   R.S.V.P.

The Secretary,
The Guild of Lacemakers,
347, Threadneedle St., E.C.2

Inserting the Names

The letters R.S.V.P. stand for *Répondez s'il vous plaît*
(answer if you please). As the French Court in pre-
revolutionary France had a reputation for elegance, this
French phrase crossed the Channel and is now standard
usage over here, perhaps because it seems more polite
than a blunt "Kindly Reply".

In the above and similar invitations, names of guests
would be inserted in the blank spaces as follows:—

The Earl and Countess of Marylebone.

Sir John and Lady Peabody.

Admiral and Mrs. Macklin.

H.E. (i.e. His Excellency) the French Ambassador
and Mme. X.

The Mayor and Mayoress of Eastchester.

The Misses Campion (i.e. 2 unmarried sisters).

Mr. and the Hon.[1] Mrs. A. C. Rosehead.

Seating Plan

At a big public dinner it is essential that the guests

---

[1] Women usually take the same rank as their husbands. But if the daughter of a
Viscount or Baron (e.g. the Honourable May Byng) marries a Commoner she is
the Hon. Mrs. —.

should know in advance where they are to sit and be able to find their way to their places without delay or confusion. It is a dinner not a treasure hunt. Usually there is one table for the more distinguished or senior members of the company, with others set at right angles to it.

The most efficient way of ensuring that guests can find their places easily is to have plans printed showing the arrangement of the tables, the 'top' table being marked A, the others B, C, and so on, each place at every table being indicated by a number, e.g. A.7.; B.2.; C.3., etc. Below the plan is given in alphabetical order the names of those attending the function, each name being followed by a letter and number indicating that person's place at a given table. As each guest enters the lobby or ante-room he is handed a copy of the seating plan.

A cheaper and less elaborate method, effective enough when the numbers are not very large, is to pin up copies of the seating plan in prominent positions in the ante-room, so that every guest can find out by studying one of these plans where he is to sit.

Name Cards at Table

At each person's place a card bearing his name should be put, corresponding, of course, to the seating arrangements as shown in the seating plan. In the case of members of the peerage it would be correct to put, say, Viscount X., and not Lord X., because the card here is equivalent to the superscription on an envelope, and not to a spoken remark addressed to him. But it would be excessive to put "the Right Hon. the Viscount X." It is scarcely necessary to add that Guests of Honour at a

function should not be required to study a plan in order
to find out where they should sit. It is the business of
their host to look after them.

Precedence at Table

A Secretary deputed to supervise the arrangements for
a public dinner would be well advised to consult his
superiors and not to arrange the seating, at all events at
the 'top' table, entirely on his own responsibility. Broadly
speaking, when members of the peerage are present,
the order of precedence would correspond with that
outlined in Chapter I and, as already mentioned, to be
found at length in *Whitaker's Almanack* and other
standard books of reference. If the principal speaker is
of lower rank than some others present he would
nevertheless (save when Royalty are also present) sit
beside the Chairman or whoever is presiding. If his wife
is also there she might be placed on the Chairman's
right with the speaker on his left. If the dinner is given
not by an individual but by a Society or other body,
then, naturally, leading members of that Society would
each have a prominent guest beside him, care being
taken to ensure that husbands and wives are not seated
together. They see plenty of one another at home and
ought therefore to welcome the opportunity, or at least
to accept the social obligation of talking to other people
at a public dinner. (It was Oscar Wilde who complained
that for a married couple to flirt with one another at
dinner was like washing one's clean linen in public).

At a reunion, such as an Old Boys' dinner, where
precedence will probably apply only to a few people
at the 'top' table, it is a good idea for the organiser
when sending out invitations to ask each recipient to

give in his reply the name of the person beside whom he would like to sit if it can be arranged.

Procedure at a Public Dinner

Grace.—At a public dinner or luncheon of any size, there is almost certain to be a clergyman present. When the guests have taken their places at the table the chairman should procure silence, by causing a gong to be struck or by some other means, and then announce: "I will call upon the Bishop of—(or whoever the senior cleric may be) to say Grace." The person concerned should be warned beforehand that he will be asked to do this. The guests will then sit down and the waiters can get to work.

Toasts.—When the final course, usually dessert or a savoury, has been cleared away, the Chairman will rise and, silence having been obtained, will propose the loyal toast, the customary formula being: "(My Lords, etc.) Ladies and Gentlemen, I give you the toast of Her Majesty the Queen."

Those present then rise and say "The Queen," raise their glasses, drink, and sit down again. Some loyalists add: "God Bless Her", but this, though doubtless unexceptionable, is not strictly correct.

After, but not before this, people may smoke. Sometimes the Chairman will give permission himself, sometimes the waiters will, without waiting for any such intimation, begin to hand round cigars and cigarettes.

Other toasts will be proposed, drunk and responded to in the same way. As each guest will probably have on the table before him a printed menu, the names of those proposing and replying to toasts can conveniently be printed on it. This is useful in so far as it informs the company what to expect. The length and quality of the speeches is—alas!—outside their control. Nevertheless, however dull a speech may be, a guest who has to leave early, should in common courtesy wait until the speech in progress has ended or, if he knows only too well what he is in for, go out unobtrusively before it begins.

Replies to Formal Invitations

An Acceptance.—Since the invitation will have been formally worded, the acceptance or refusal of it will be in the same style as the invitation. The form admits of some variations, but the following is usual:—

> Sir John and Lady Sturtevant
> or Dr. and Mrs. Bullard
> ,, The Bishop of Barchester and Mrs. Proudie
> ,, Mrs. Fry and the Misses Fry

have great pleasure in accepting the kind invitation of the Master and Fellows of St. Cyprian's College to dinner on Wednesday, 30th October, at 7.45 p.m.

It is always wise to mention the date and hour in the reply, so that if the writer has misread the invitation or put the wrong date or time owing to a slip of the pen, his prospective hosts can point this out and so ensure that he does not arrive at the wrong time or on the wrong day. G. K. Chesterton, it is said, was so vague that he would telephone to his wife, saying: "I'm in Birmingham, where ought I to be?" He was doubtless forgiven such lapses, but we ought not to err in the same way, and it is simple enough to avoid it.

A Refusal.—The standard form is as follows:

Major and Mrs. Buckley greatly regret that, owing to a previous engagement, they are unable to accept the kind invitation of the Master and Fellows of St. Cyprian's College to dinner on Wednesday, 30th October. (As the couple are not coming there is no point in mentioning the time of the dinner.)

The phrase "owing to a previous engagement" may be a genuine excuse. On the other hand it may mean that the couple have no wish to come. But it would obviously be rude to say so, and to include this conventional phrase lessens the bluntness of the refusal. For all that, if the invitation is to a small dinner party given by personal friends, it is better to state the nature of the previous engagement, for the very reason that the conventional phrase may seem slightly unfriendly. Nevertheless, it is better to use it than to invent an alleged prior engagement, since the deception might be found out with embarrassing consequences.

Invitations to a Private Dinner-Party

If the host and hostess are in the habit of entertaining their friends fairly frequently, and expect to have a dozen or more at their table, they would send out printed invitations in the usual form, namely:—

Mr. and Mrs. Siddons
request the pleasure of
(Mr. and Mrs. David Garrick's)
company at Dinner
on Thursday, 6th January, at 8 o'clock.

7, Drury Lane, W.C.2.   R.S.V.P.

An acceptance would be in the form already given. A refusal, in the standard form, would be quite correct, but might, alternatively, be worded as follows:—

Mr. and Mrs. David Garrick are extremely sorry that they are unable to accept the kind invitation of Mr. and

Mrs. Siddons to dinner on 6th January, as they have already arranged to go away and will not be back until the middle of the month.

An Invitation at Short Notice

Invitations to a dinner party should be sent out in good time. Hosts aim at having an equal number of men and women at their table. If, owing to illness or some

other reason, one of those invited has to cry off at short notice, the host will want to fill the gap so as to even up the numbers again. This situation has to be handled with tact. A person of eminence or pomposity (the two do not necessarily go together) might resent being invited as, so to speak, an afterthought. The best thing in these circumstances therefore is to enlist the help of an old friend who, because he is an old friend, will not take offence. The hostess might therefore ring him up or, if she writes, do so in some such way as this:—

(My) dear ——

We have known you for a long time, so may I

claim the privilege of an old friend and ask whether you could possibly dine with us on Friday night? We are giving a dinner party and one of our guests has been rushed off to hospital. I do hope you will forgive this very unceremonious invitation, but if you do chance to be free that night (Dinner at 8 o'clock) and could help us out by coming at such short notice, not only should we be delighted to see you, but you would be rendering a real service to

Yours very sincerely,

Nora Holmes.

Invitations to Sherry Parties, etc.

The simplest way of sending out invitations of this kind is to make use of cards, readily obtainable from stationers, and blank save for the words "At Home" printed in the centre, and for the initials R.S.V.P. in the lower right hand corner. Across the top of the card the hostess writes in the names of the people to whom that card is to be sent, her own name above the words "At Home" and adds the necessary details.

The complete card, which should be sent in an envelope, would read as follows:—

Mr. and Mrs. Geoffrey Evans

Mrs. Somers

"At Home"

Saturday, 5th July.

Sherry.   R.S.V.P.

6—7.30 p.m.   Dunton House,

Guildford.

The advantage of this method is that it gives the necessary information in relatively few words. Moreover, the printed cards can be used for other invitations than to sherry, since on some other occasion a similar card might bear in the left-hand bottom corner the words: Dancing, 8—11 p.m.: Music, 8—10 p.m., or whatever entertainment a hostess may have in mind.

It is important to include the later as well as the earlier limit of time, otherwise the guests are in the awkward position of not knowing whether they are causing inconvenience by staying too long. To any such invitation the acceptance or refusal would be worded in the third person in the usual way.

Informal Invitations

Under this heading come friendly invitations extended to one person or one or more married couples to lunch, dinner, tea or, say, to play tennis. A formal, third person invitation would not be intimate enough. If the hosts are a married couple, the wife would write the letter of invitation and, if she proposes to invite another married couple to lunch would address her letter and the envelope to the woman, not the man, in, for example, the following terms:—

> 16, Broad Street,
> Edgeways,
> 21st August.

Dear Mrs. Spencer,

It would give us a great deal of pleasure if you and your husband would dine with us on Thursday, 31st August at 8 o'clock. There would only be the four of us, and we hope very much that you may be able to come.

> Yours sincerely,
> Esther Marks.

The Reply.
27, High Street,
Shortleigh,
23rd August.

Dear Mrs. Marks,

How very kind of you. My husband and I will be delighted to dine with you next Thursday (31st August) at 8 o'clock.

Yours sincerely,
Jennifer Spencer.

Or:—

Dear Mrs. Marks,

Thank you very much for your kind invitation for next Thursday, which we are very sorry indeed to have to decline. My husband has to be at a meeting that evening and so, to our great disappointment, we shall not be able to come.

Yours sincerely,
Jennifer Spencer.

Invitations to weddings may be conveniently dealt with later in this book. Meanwhile we may consider some of the duties and responsibilities of hosts and guests at dinner parties and other gatherings, specimen invitations to which have been given in this chapter.

CHAPTER IV

ENTERTAINING AT HOME

Duties of Hosts: Dinner Parties

Dress.—Unless someone is genuinely unconventional he is likely to feel acutely embarrassed if, on coming to a dinner-party, he finds that he is dressed differently from all the other men present. Women, likewise, though usually much better than men at carrying off such a situation, also very naturally like to know what they are expected to wear.

Very often, there is no doubt. A man receiving an invitation to dinner, especially one worded in the third person, would certainly assume that he was expected to wear evening dress. But it may not always be clear whether he should wear full evening dress or a black tie and a dinner jacket. In cases of doubt it is more complimentary to one's hosts to be over than under dressed, but a considerate hostess may set a man's mind at rest in advance by putting the words 'Black Tie' or 'White Tie', or something of the sort on the invitation card. Such an indication would also enable his wife to decide what sort of dress she should wear for the occasion. Nowadays, in private houses and except when the members of the party intend after dinner to go on to, say, a Hunt Ball, a dinner jacket is more usual than full evening dress.

Introductions Before Dinner.—The hosts who, presumably, know all their guests, for otherwise they would not have invited them, should not take it for granted that all their guests already know each other. The interval between the arrival of the guests and going into dinner should not be longer than about twenty minutes. All the guests are unlikely to arrive simultaneously, but they will probably do so within a few minutes of one another. Incidentally, when sending out invitations it is often useful to put on the card 7.45 p.m. (for 8 o'clock), thus making it clear that dinner will be served at eight, but that guests are expected to arrive 10 or 15 minutes earlier than that. It is the business of the host and hostess to greet them when they are shown into the drawing-room, or wherever they are received and, usually, to offer them a glass of sherry or a cocktail. If the guests do not number more than eight or ten, it should during this time be perfectly possible for the host and hostess to introduce them all to one another.[1]

The hostess will have arranged in advance who is to sit next to whom and it is the responsibility of the host, whatever else he may lack the opportunity to do, to introduce each man to the lady he is "to take into dinner", in other words to the lady who will be sitting beside him.

If the number of guests is small the host may still find it helpful to have a plan of the table, so that he can indicate to each man the places which he and the lady he is taking in are to occupy.

Seating Arrangements.—Even at a small dinner-party of ten or twelve people the seating arrangements are governed to some extent by precedence. Usually the host will occupy one end of the table, his wife or, if he is single, the lady whom he has asked to act as hostess for the occasion, the other end.

[1] See *Introductions* on page 42.

The lady who is senior in rank or, failing that, in age or social position, sits on the right hand of the host, the corresponding male on the left of the hostess. This may complete what we may term the compulsory placings. But if two other guests are clearly entitled to the second most important places, then the lady concerned should sit on the left hand of the host, the man on the right hand of the hostess.

Another point to bear in mind is that husbands and wives should not sit immediately next to one another. Sometimes it is useful to put cards bearing the occupant's name on the table opposite each chair, but if the guests are few and the host has already had a word on this subject with the men, he can dispense with cards and from his place at the head of the table direct his guests to their proper places as they enter the dining-room.

Common sense may dictate some modification of the seating plan. If the host knows that two people have tastes in common or are old friends who have not met for a long time, he may decide to arrange for them to sit together. Conversely, if he suspects that two others cordially detest one another and that the most to be hoped for between them is an armed truce, he will separate them as far as other considerations allow. He would do even better not to invite them both on the same evening, for veiled hostility between two of the number may well mar the enjoyment of the rest.

Going in to Dinner.—The advantage of proceeding to the dining-room in a prescribed order is that it prevents people from hovering in front of the door like an un-usually diffident bus-queue. The disadvantage is that, if too firmly insisted on, the occasion may be made more formal than is desired. For this reason the host, having assured himself that each man knows which lady he is to take in may leave the couples to go in to dinner in any order they choose. But if one or two of the guests are clearly more socially prominent than the rest, it may be wiser to abide by the rules of precedence. In that case the host should lead the way, offering his right arm to the lady who will sit on his right hand at table. The chief male guest will follow in the same way with his hostess, unless she decides, as sometimes happens, to bring up the rear, allowing the remaining couples to go in ahead of her.

Wines at Dinner.—At a large public dinner or similar function, a wide variety of wines are sometimes served, sherry being offered with the soup, a white wine, Sauterne or Chablis, with the fish, champagne or claret or burgundy with game or meat courses, with a choice of port or claret with the dessert. All this, though doubtless very agreeable, is costly and a trifle ostentatious at a private dinner-party. It is quite sufficient to offer sherry with the soup, white wine with the fish, and a choice of the same white wine or claret with the main course. Alternatively, after the sherry, hock could be served throughout the meal, that is, until dessert is on the table. Again, champagne could be served with no other wine at all until dessert. Skilled advice could, no doubt, be obtained from knowledgeable friends or reputable wine-merchants, but in general it is much better to provide a sound, if modest, table wine than, say, inferior champagne. It is also desirable to bear in mind that many people—despite the avidity with which they partake of trifle with sherry in it—are teetotallers (To Hell with Burgundy!) or, even if they are not, many for reasons of health, drink wine sparingly or not at all.

Hence the need to have water, orangeade or lemonade available. It is embarrassing if a guest asks for a soft drink and finds that none has been provided. Again, while every opportunity should be given for glasses to be refilled, it is inconsiderate for hosts, out of a mistaken sense of hospitality, to press wine on guests when they really do not want any more, or to be offended when they refuse. Besides, the guest knows how much he can drink with impunity better than the host!

Menus for Dinner-Parties.—This is not a cookery book. Therefore it is purely as examples that there follow two specimen menus, one suitable for the summer, the other for the winter.

Summer	Winter
Grape Fruit.	Clear Soup (Julienne)
Boiled Salmon (Hollandaise Sauce).	Boiled Turbot (Shrimp Sauce).
Roast Chicken (Bread Sauce).	Lamb Cutlets (Mint Sauce).
with Peas and Potatoes.	Brussels Sprouts, Potatoes.
Fruit Salad and/or Meringues.	Trifle and/or Wine Jelly.
Mushrooms on Toast.	Cheese Soufflé.
Dessert.	Dessert.
Coffee.	Coffee.

It is usual for a few copies of the menu, either typed or else in handwriting to be place on the table, but one for every two or three guests is sufficient.[1]

"*Shall We Join the Ladies*."—When dinner is over and a few minutes have elapsed since the port (or claret as an alternative choice) has been round the table for the first time, it is customary for the ladies to leave and go

[1] For some remarks on table manners, see page 175.

to the drawing-room.[1] The hostess, waiting for a lull in the conversation, catches the eye of the lady on the host's right and gets up, the others following suit. The men likewise rise, the one nearest the door opening it for the ladies to go out. Left to themselves the men, at the invitation of their host, move up to one end of the table, so that they can talk and smoke more conveniently. The decanters of port and claret are on the table (the servants having gone out), and the host should see that they are passed round *in a clockwise direction*, though the superstition behind this injunction is obscure. In the old days of heroic drinkers, this male session was lengthy. Nowadays, after about twenty minutes, the host should, possibly with the time-honoured phrase: "Shall we join the ladies?", indicate that it is time to move.

It is also—let us be practical—a suitable time to enable his guests to 'wash their hands' (though it is to be hoped that the host will refrain from using such phrases as "you know the geography of the house" and the like).

Moving Guests Round.—The ladies meanwhile will have been drinking coffee[2] and, if the men have not had theirs at table, they may be offered it when they enter the drawing-room. The host's main duty at this stage is to see that, so far as possible, each guest, who has hitherto talked chiefly with his neighbour at table, should have a chance to converse with others. During dinner a given couple may have exhausted their topics of conversation and, even if they have not, it is unreasonable that one person should monopolise another throughout the evening. The host therefore should say to one man "I

---

[1] This has nothing to do with 'drawing', but is really the 'withdrawing room'.
[2] If they have not already had it in the dining-room with the men.

don't think you've had a talk with Mrs. X yet," or something of the sort. He can then either take the place vacated himself or bring a third man up to occupy it. When the total numbers do not exceed a dozen or so, it should not be difficult to ensure that each man has a few minutes conversation with each lady.

During this after-dinner period it is a good idea to have available on a side-table a supply of soft drinks, and possibly whisky and soda, to be offered, not immediately, but half an hour or so after the men have 'joined the ladies.'

If the host and hostess have thus played their parts they have done their best to make the evening a success. If it has not turned out well, the fault will not be theirs. But the guests, too, have their responsibilities.

Duties of Guests at Dinner-Parties

Punctuality.—Any housewife knows that when food is 'done to a turn', as the phrase goes, it tends to lose its perfection if not served at approximately the hour planned. This holds good also at a dinner-party and provides one very good reason why guests should arrive punctually. Another is that, especially if all the guests are not already acquainted with one another, there is likely to be at first a certain constraint. Consequently, the shorter the period before going in to dinner the better. Therefore if the guests are invited to dine at 8 o'clock, they should do their utmost, despite tardiness of taxis, missing collar studs, laddered stockings and the general cussedness of things, not to be late. If the invitation states 7.45 for 8 o'clock they should aim at arriving not before but very shortly after the earlier time limit.

Before Dinner.—If, on arriving at the house, a man is asked to leave his hat and coat in the hall, while his wife is directed by a servant to some other room, the man should wait until his wife reappears, so that they may both greet their hosts together. If there is a servant to announce them, the man should give their names (Mr. and Mrs. X, "Sir John and Lady Y") in distinct, but not stentorian tones. Having shaken hands with their host and hostess (a formality that may sometimes be dispensed with between host and a male guest who know each other well), the newly arrived couple should shake hands with or bow to others in the room whom they may know.

In particular the man should seek out the lady whom his host informs him he is to take into dinner. If he can (without too much insincerity and fortified by sherry) tell the lady in question how pleased he is by this prospect, he will have begun the evening as a good guest should.

At Dinner.—On reaching the dinner-table, the man should not sit down until the lady he is taking in has done so. He should, indeed, draw back her chair for her, but there is no need to be obsequious about it.

Conversation.—It is the man's business to converse mainly with the lady he has taken in, for it is not usually possible to talk across the table to any extent, but he should not neglect the lady on his left. This does not mean, of course, that the lady should not initiate topics of conversation herself. On the contrary, each should contribute to keeping the conversation going. If one subject strikes no responsive chord, another should be tried. It is damping if someone either out of shyness, bad temper or sheer rudeness kills every topic dead with a chilly monosyllable. On the other hand conversation is essentially an exchange of ideas, not a monologue and, unless one or the other is driven in desperation to discourse at length because the other will say nothing, long-windedness is to be deplored.

It may be that one party to a conversation knows that the other is an authority on some subject and, being genuinely interested in what he has to say, need therefore do no more than make an occasional comment. The said expert should, however, bear in mind that the next course cannot be served until everyone has finished the one before, so he should not talk so continuously as to court indigestion by having to gobble what is on his plate because everybody else has already finished.

No rules, of course, will influence a notorious and incorrigible bore. People less chronically verbose should endeavour to draw their partner out, not forgetting to address occasional remarks to the person in the other adjacent chair, particularly if its occupant seems to be finding conversation difficult with his or her other neighbour. But it is inconsiderate to intervene in this way if a flourishing conversation is already in progress. A guest, in short, should pull his conversational weight, but not throw his weight about.

Things One Can't Eat.—If hot soup gives you hiccoughs, you hate oysters and cannot swallow trifle with bananas lurking in it, what should one do?

The obvious comment is that one individual who dislikes all these is exceptionally unlucky if he is faced with all of them at the same dinner. The dilemma is, nevertheless, a real one, except at a big public dinner where one can obviously refuse one or more dishes without offending one's hostess. It becomes most acute for a guest—perhaps the only one—at a family table. Then, there is no perfect solution. If you are old friends, frank admission of one's dislike may be the best method. Alternatively one can plead lack of appetite or that one has already partaken so lavishly of the excellent preceding courses that a very little will suffice. At a private dinner-party at least some of the dishes will be proffered by a servant, so the cautious guest, who has his suspicions, can help himself to as little as he likes. With others he can toy discreetly with what is on his plate. No reasonable hostess could object to this, though she might make a mental note for future reference to the effect that Mrs. R. doesn't like salmon mayonnaise.

Sometimes people are on a diet. At a hotel or restaurant they can choose dishes to suit themselves. At a private dinner-party common politeness demands that they should accept what their hosts offer, even though it may mean making a mere pretence rather than a reality of eating. After all, if they are really so fussy as to believe that a piece of pheasant will prove fatal, or a potato bring on appoplexy, they should not have accepted the invitation in the first place.

When to Go.—Stephen Leacock (Is he much read nowadays?) wrote a nice story about a shy young curate who was invited to tea by one of the parishioners. Too diffident to take his leave, he stayed to supper and, as he still showed no disposition to depart, the host had to put him up for the night. Thereafter, his nerve broken, the curate stayed wretchedly on, fell into a decline after a few weeks, and took to his bed in the spare room. At last he raised himself on his pillows, murmured with a seraphic smile the words that had so long eluded him: "I think I must be going now," and passed peacefully away.

Hosts, presumably, do not really have to offer such extended hospitality. But they do undeniably suffer from the inability of some people to know when to go. At a Sherry party or a dance the host can indicate on the invitation card the proposed duration of the function. At a dinner-party, on the other hand, the initiative rests with the guests.

There can be no rigid rule, but an approximate time of departure is readily arrived at. If the company go into dinner at 8 o'clock the meal, that is until the ladies withdraw, could be expected to occupy about 75 minutes. If the men sit by themselves for 20 minutes or so, they will rejoin the ladies at about 9.35 p.m. or soon after. Therefore, some 50 minutes later, say, 10.30 p.m. would be a suitable time for the guests to leave. Strictly, it rests with the senior lady, i.e. the one who has sat on the host's right hand at dinner, to make the first move. But if she fails to take the lead it would be perfectly proper for someone else to do so and, normally, all the guests would leave together. Sometimes one of them will have ordered a taxi for 10.30 p.m. and its arrival could therefore provide the occasion for a general move.

Assuming that there are servants to help the guests into their coats, the hostess will probably say good-bye to them in the drawing-room and remain there. The host may elect to accompany them to the front door. If he does, do not embark on a long story, however funny, on the doorstep. You have an overcoat on and he has not. Guests who have cars or taxis should ask those unprovided with either whether they "would like a lift home," an offer which can be accepted with a clear conscience provided that it does not involve the person making it in going a very considerable distance out of his way.

Fashions change. But even today it does not come amiss if guests, having thanked their hosts by word of mouth on taking their leave, write next day to express their appreciation again.

Duties of Servants at Private Dinner-Parties

In these days when very many people have no servants at all or rely on a 'daily help' (who may, in fact, come only two or three times a week), there is a certain unreality about this section. Where there is no domestic help at all or very little, hospitality is necessarily informal, with the guests as likely as not lending a hand with the washing-up.

Nevertheless, dinner-parties of the kind described do take place, though more rarely than formerly, and, as they cannot be arranged without adequate domestic help, either permanent, temporary or hired for the occasion, something should be said briefly about the duties of servants at dinner-parties of the sort with which this chapter has been concerned.

Arrival and Departure of Guests.—The exact allocation of duties depends on the number of servants available. Ideally, one should open the door to the arriving guests and take charge of the men's hats and coats, while another looks after the ladies. The former should also conduct the guests to where their hosts are waiting to receive them, and announce their names in a voice loud enough to be heard above the murmur of conversation that may be in progress in the room. The same servant, or another, should then offer sherry or cocktails on a tray before the party go in to dinner. Similarly at the end of the evening one or more servants should be on hand to help the departing guests into their coats and to see them out.

At Dinner.—A man entertaining one or two friends to a meal will probably have the joint placed before him and do the carving[1] himself, the servant, if there is one, taking each plate from him in turn, and handing the vegetables round.

At the kind of dinner we are considering however, a servant will serve the soup from a tureen, placed on a side-table or elsewhere, another taking the plates as they are filled and putting one in turn at each place at the table. The fish, game, cutlets or joint will, either in the kitchen or at a side-table, be arranged in portions in a dish, so that each person can help himself when it is offered to him, the servant presenting it to the left, not the right, hand side of the guest. If vegetables or sauces are not in the same dish as the fish, or whatever the dish

---

[1] "The trouble with goose," as one unskilled performer remarked plaintively, "is that the gravy so seldom matches the wallpaper."

contains, another servant should follow up quickly with them, so that the service is smooth.

Strictly, the first person to be served is the lady on the host's right, next the one on his left, followed by the remaining guests on that side, and so round the table back to the host. If several servants are available one of them can, at the same time, start with the man on the hostess's right and then work to the left.

As soon as all have been served with a particular course, one of the servants can serve the wine, asking each guest which he would prefer if there is a choice. When a glass is empty or nearly so the servant should prepare to refill it, leaving it to the guest to say "No, thank you," if he so wishes.

At the end of the meal, that is when the ladies have withdrawn or, at least, when the port decanter is on the table and perhaps coffee has been served, the servants go out, only returning when the men have joined the ladies to clear away.

Such, with variations according to the size of the party and the number of the domestic staff, is the usual procedure.

Sherry and Cocktail Parties

At a luncheon or dinner-party in a private house the number of guests is usually small: in a flat it is likely to be smaller still. The same applies to tea-parties, which have the added disadvantages of being less festive than either, and of taking place at a time when professional or domestic duties render it difficult for people to come.

Sherry or Cocktail parties, on the other hand, provide a form of entertainment which has much to commend it. They are easier to arrange than luncheons or dinners. They do not last long, usually only from 6—7.30 p.m. and such a time is suitable whether a guest comes almost straight from work or "looks in" for a short while on the way to dinner elsewhere. Moreover, as most guests at such affairs usually stand rather than sit, it is possible to entertain, even in a small flat, a comparatively large number of people at one time. Again, if one has been invited to dinner by people considerably better off than oneself, one may not be able to return their hospitality in the same way or on the same scale. A Cocktail party provides a means of doing so at least in some measure.

Duties of Hosts.—Although a Cocktail party is a comparatively simple form of entertainment, this does not mean that careful planning is unnecessary. No party can be counted a success if the guests are so tightly packed together that they can scarcely move, only a fortunate few can get anywhere near the drinks, and if a newcomer, fighting his or her way into the throng, has the impression of being in a stifling and unusually raucous parrot-house.

By moving some of the furniture into another room, but leaving against the walls a few chairs for the older guests, a substantial space in the middle can be cleared. But the hosts should remember that their guests want to be able to circulate instead of having to talk solely to the person they chance to be next to, and that space must be allowed for trays of food and drink to be carried about with reasonable ease. The numbers should therefore be calculated with these considerations in mind. For this reason it is prudent to compile in the first instance a list of people who 'must be invited', and not to send out invitations to others until refusals from some of those on the list have been received.

People who have a fairly large house (with perhaps a garden into which the guests can overflow if the weather is fine) may decide to give one really large party, with a hundred or more guests. In that case they will probably be wise to entrust all the arrangements to a reputable catering firm at an agreed charge per head. In that event the caterers will provide glasses, plates and cutlery, etc.

as well as food and drink. This takes the bulk of the work off the hostess's shoulders, but she will probably still be responsible for outside arrangements, in particular for posting someone to show guests where they can leave their cars. If the parking place is in the street, not in the grounds of the house, it would be well to consult the local police beforehand, and perhaps to ask for the services of a constable while the party is in progress. A guest's gratitude to his host is likely to be considerably lessened if, on leaving the house, he is faced with a summons for parking his car in the wrong place.

EGM—C*

For a smaller party the host and his family will doubtless rely on their own resources, supplemented by such domestic assistance as they may have. If there is only one maid, she can probably be best employed in admitting the guests, taking charge of their hats and coats, and directing them into the room. Either the host or hostess should, at least while the majority of the guests are arriving, stand near the door of the room where the party is being held, in order to greet them. If there is no domestic help at all, the front door of the house or flat can be left open or have a notice affixed to it requesting the guests to make their way in. The reason for this is that, with a party in progress, the babel of conversation is likely to drown the ringing of the door-bell.

What to Provide.—What the host decides to offer his guests is largely a matter of choice and financial means. Some people provide sherry, others cocktails of several kinds as well. In either case soft drinks, such as orange juice or tomato juice should be available. The eatables may consist of some or all of the following:—sandwiches of various kinds (e.g. egg, ham, cheese), small sausages transfixed by sticks of the sort used for cherries in cocktails, cheese straws, potato crisps, and biscuits or rounds of bread adorned with shrimps, anchovies and the like.

Whatever is provided, a supply should be laid out beforehand on plates or dishes. Glasses of the various drinks should likewise be in readiness on trays. Failing this, if a number of guests arrive hard on each other's heels, there will be undue delay in providing them all with something to eat and drink. Where there is little or no domestic help, the hostess should enlist the aid of close friends with suitably steady hands to help hand round.

No one has yet devised the perfect method of disposing of the sticks used to transfix cherries and sausages after they have fulfilled their purpose, with the result that they find their way into fireplaces and flowerpots. But they can be deposited on ashtrays, and a hostess should have a number of these dotted about, because with a cigarette in their hands, otherwise well-conducted persons sometimes show a deplorable disregard for carpets and chair covers.

The problem of moving guests about on these occasions is difficult. A thoughtful hostess will make a note beforehand to introduce to each other certain people who are not acquainted and who, she thinks, are likely to get on well together. If some individual is standing disconsolately alone and another is having a prolonged session with an accomplished bore, she should come to the rescue. But if people are obviously happy in each other's company it is a mistake to disturb them. Fussiness in a hostess is as much a fault as negligence. Besides, the remedy often rests with the guests.

Duties of Guests at a Sherry Party

There is not a great deal to be said under this heading, since a Sherry party demands the same civility and good manners as any other social occasion. It is important, however, that invitations to a Sherry party should be answered promptly in order that the hostess may know in good time how many people to expect, and also be able, if she wishes, to invite others if some of those originally invited are unable to come. When they arrive guests should greet their hostess and walk past her into the room, not band together near the door so that newcomers cannot get by. Secondly, while guests may prefer to talk to close friends at the party, they should be prepared to make new acquaintances, and to accept with a good grace their hostess's suggestions that she should introduce them to somebody else. Further, if the party is a small one and domestic help lacking, a man might very well ask his hostess whether she would like him to hand round drinks. If a man finds himself next to another, whom he does not know, he can address some remark to him without waiting to be introduced. He should not attempt to join in a conversation already in progress between two or more people, but should leave it to them to bring him into it, if they wish. A man finding himself standing beside a girl, who appears to be alone and whom he does not know, may be doing a kindness to her and beginning an acquaintanceship which will give pleasure to him, by offering to get her something to eat or drink. If she wishes, she can then herself begin to talk to him, but he should not force his acquaintance upon her. If a man knows that a particular girl is there whom he would like to know, he should try to get his hostess, or someone else, to introduce him to her. If this is not practicable and he happens to know that the girl and himself have a mutual friend, he can legitimately seek her out, saying: "My name's X, I believe you know So and So, who's an old friend of mine," or something of the kind.

One last point. If an invitation card bears the words 6—7.30 p.m. any guest can come or leave within the limits of time. But he should not arrive before 6 o'clock or stay later than 7.30 p.m.

Staying with Friends

The assumption here is that hosts and guests are

close friends. They therefore understand one another and have no need to study each other's likes and dislikes, as acquaintances would need to do. In such circumstances a hostess need not cudgel her brains in the hope of hitting on something that the guests would like to do. Any suggestions can be freely discussed, and neither party will be offended if the guests have plans of their own.

For all that, guests should show themselves considerate, however close their relations with their hosts. In particular, they should be punctual, avoid causing unnecessary work in the house, say in good time whether they intend to be in or out for a meal, and leave their hostess in no doubt either of the date and time of their arrival or of when they intend to leave. For their part a couple, proposing to invite friends to stay and having a definite programme in mind for them, should make this plain when writing to invite them. The guests in Noel Coward's *Hay Fever* had a ghastly time because they did not know what they were in for. If someone regards participation in private theatricals with dread, and looks on charades as a foretaste of hell, it is unfair to spring such activities on him, or to coerce him into taking part when he is clearly reluctant to do so. There is the additional and practical point that guests need to know in advance whether they are expected to bring, say, golf clubs, or are likely to need full evening dress.

Putting Up an Acquaintance

This is a more delicate matter for both host and guest. Fortunately the ordeal, should it prove to be one for either, is likely to be brief—a matter of one or two nights only, for an acquaintance or a virtual stranger would surely be invited for a particular occasion, or at least only for a short visit. It would be foolish to extend and rash to accept prolonged hospitality when host and guest know each other slightly or not at all.

It may be that the guest is coming down for a tennis-tournament or a dance, to give a lecture, attend a meeting or preach a sermon. If he intends to come by car and the route is not straightforward, the host should send him directions. If he is coming by rail, the host should, if possible, be at the station or arrange for him to be met.

It is always difficult to know to what extent such casual acquaintances require to be entertained. Some fit in without difficulty into the routine of the family, others less well.

There are no hard and fast rules. It is worth remarking, however, that particularly when the guest has come to speak or preach, his notion of true hospitality is very likely to be left to his own devices, free to think over what he has to say, to read, or to take things quietly before the evening's engagement. The said guest, his speech or sermon over, should not, for his part, keep his hosts up to all hours. It is difficult for a man to go to bed leaving his guest still up. The latter should therefore take himself off at a reasonable hour, and will be the more likely to do so if the hostess has had the forethought to put readable books, not the ones that nobody else wants, in the spare room.

Any guest staying only for a night or two ought to go fairly soon after breakfast on the day of his departure and not, without good reason, interfere with the normal family routine by remaining until after lunch. The host, on his side, should make things easy for his guest by getting him to the station in good time. True, he knows better than his guest how long it takes to reach the station, but some hosts, oblivious of their companion's anxiety, take a curious pride in driving up just as the train comes to a halt at the platform.

It is scarcely necessary to add that a guest in a private house should tip the maid who has looked after him, and write a note of thanks, a "bread-and-butter letter", to his hostess. It need not be long or effusive, but it should be posted promptly, not as a belated afterthought. It might run as follows:

Dear Mrs. ——

It was extremely good of you to entertain me so hospitably last night. You made my stay very enjoyable, and I greatly appreciate your kindness, as well as the opportunity it gave me to see something of the very pleasant home in which you live.

With kind regards and, again, many thanks.

Yours sincerely,
Roger Barrington.

CHAPTER V

ENTERTAINING OUTSIDE THE HOME—
ETIQUETTE OUT OF DOORS

Entertaining in Restaurants, etc.

To lunch or dine in a restaurant usually costs more than to have a meal at home, and the larger the number of people the greater the proportionate difference in expense is likely to be. Nevertheless there are times when the convenience and enjoyment of this form of hospitality make up for the additional expense incurred.

The occasion may be a wedding anniversary or a birthday party. It may be a question of meeting business associates to whom for ulterior motives one wishes to give a more lavish dinner than one could do at home. Again, it may well be that a wife, heartily sick of the sight of the kitchen sink, informs her husband that it is high time they had an evening out. "And what about the So-and-So's? We've owed them a meal for ages, and besides it would be fun!"

Whatever the precise reason the important thing is that the occasion should prove to be an enjoyable one.

Duties of the Host.—The burden of catering is lifted from the shoulders of the host who entertains his friends at a restaurant instead of at home, but his obligations are still more than purely financial. To begin with, unless he proposes himself to collect the guests by car or taxi he must satisfy himself that they know exactly where and at what time they are expected to turn up and, if he is inviting them to dinner, whether they are to wear evening dress or not. Uncertainty on any of these points can wreck an evening from the start. If it has been agreed that the guests are to be at a certain restaurant at a particular time, the host (and the hostess) must be there before the guests. A wise host will naturally choose a restaurant where he knows the meals are good and well-served, and if he has even the slightest reason for supposing that the place selected may be full, he should ring up in advance and book a table, stating his name, the number of people and the time at which the meal is to begin. If the restaurant has an orchestra he may, at his discretion, ask for a table some little distance from it, for not everyone relishes over-obtrusive Offenbach with the oysters or too resounding a rumba with the roast.

Before the Meal.—Adjacent to or leading into the restaurant or hotel dining-room there will probably be a bar or lounge where the host and his guests will meet. Unless time is short, perhaps because the party propose to go on to a theatre afterwards, the host should offer sherry or cocktails and, while these are being served, he might usefully have a word with the waiter at the door of the restaurant to make sure that the table he has reserved is available. If it is not, he may prompt that dignitary with the aid of a tip to come over and tell him when the table is ready for them.

Usually when approaching a door a man will step aside to allow a lady to go ahead of him or open it for her. But when a man is entertaining friends in a restaurant it would be proper for him to go in first, so that he may attract the attention of the head-waiter, who will conduct the party to their table.

Ordering the Meal.—At most hotels and restaurants guests may choose between a set menu (*Table d'hôte*) for luncheon or dinner and a wider range of dishes to be selected *à la carte*. The set meal is likely to be somewhat cheaper and can usually be more speedily served. The waiter will probably put a menu before each guest, but the host, without endeavouring to influence their choice in any way, may fairly be expected to give them a lead. Even in the *table d'hôte* meal there is likely to be some choice, e.g. thick *or* clear soup, cutlets *or* chicken, etc., so the first thing for him to do is to find out whether the set meal will meet his guests' tastes, or whether they would prefer to lunch or dine *à la carte*. If the former, each guest has merely to state his choice from the limited alternatives available. If the latter, the host may make a few suggestions and encourage his guests to put forward their own. If the establishment is known to make a speciality of certain dishes he may well draw attention to them. The guests, for their part, should remember that *à la carte* dishes may take some time to prepare. They should therefore order them at the beginning of the meal and not suddenly ask for one when the soup and fish have already been served. Considerate guests will likewise think twice before asking for the most expensive dishes on the bill of fare, though they may safely do so if the host chooses them for himself or if they know that he is well off.

Not long ago it was thought very ill-bred to express appreciation of the food placed before one. War-time rationing and subsequent austerity have largely dispelled this attitude. Admittedly, gluttony is a vice, but on the other hand it is no compliment to one's host's hospitality or to a restaurant that takes a pride in its cuisine to appear completely indifferent to what one eats. There is, after all, a middle course between apathetically accepting anything remotely edible on the one hand and smacking one's chops over the menu on the other. Nowadays no hostess would be likely to take it amiss if she were complimented on the dinner she had provided. In Scandinavia, indeed, it is customary for one of the guests in a private house to rise at the end of the meal and pay courteous tribute to her on behalf of his fellow guests and himself.

Ordering Wines.—Some wines are expensive. Therefore, when he studies the wine-list put into his hands by the wine waiter, the host, in fairness to his guests, must give them a clue. On their side they should be prepared to follow it, but they need a hint from him to which they can respond. If he is a rich man, or if the occasion is a special one and extravagance therefore justified, he can make his position clear by jovially suggesting champagne. But he must do this with conviction, not with an ill-disguised anxiety betraying a devout hope that the suggestion will be turned down!

If neither his circumstances, the occasion (nor, perhaps, his expenses account) warrant such lavishness, he should say: "Well, what would you like to drink? What about some hock, or would you prefer burgundy?" The guests then know where they are in the matter. The ladies, whose views he should ask in the first place, can then express their preference, though they will possibly leave the decision to the men, in the belief, flattering but often unfounded, that they know more about it. If there is a knowledgeable male guest, the host may be well advised to defer to his opinion. Failing that, he should make his own decision. Having decided on the kind of wine, he may very well consult the wine waiter. There is a risk that the latter will seize the opportunity to get rid of a bottle of some inferior brand which the management, in a misguided moment, had bought cheap at a sale. It is far more likely, however, that the waiter will respond to an appeal for skilled advice by recommending a wine good in itself and suitable for drinking with the dishes that have been ordered.

When he serves the wine he will first pour a little into the host's glass and, only when the latter has sipped and approved it, will he fill the guest's glasses and then the host's. If the wine is 'corked' or otherwise unsatisfactory the host is entitled to draw the waiter's attention to its condition and, if the complaint is justified, another bottle will be provided instead. Admittedly it requires some moral courage to make a complaint, but a man who is a judge of wine is fully entitled to do so, though it is seldom necessary.

Tipping.—At restaurants in this country it is unusual for a fixed charge for service to be included in the bill. When at the end of a meal the host calls for his bill, the waiter will bring it to him folded in half on a plate. Max Beerbohm, describing himself as by nature a guest rather than a host, remarked in an essay that at sight of the bill he was always filled with panic lest he should not have enough money to meet it, and had to fight against the temptation to open it immediately so as to know the worst at once.

The perfect host would, no doubt, leave it on the plate for a few minutes, then glance at it calmly without interrupting his conversation. The perfect guest, for his part, would continue to talk casually to other guests while his host was actually paying the bill, and certainly refrain from looking to see how much money his host puts down, and what he leaves on the plate for a tip!

We cannot all play the host with negligent ease, but we can at least deal adequately with the problem of tipping. The rough working rule is that the tip should be not less and not much more than 10% of the amount of the bill. Thus, if the bill comes to say, £3/15/0 (10% of which is 7/6) it would be rather niggardly to give the waiter £4, and proper to give him £4/2/6 or £4/5/0 or as near to it as the loose change in one's pocket allows.

Sometimes the bill is presented, not by the waiter who has actually served you, but by one more exalted. There may be some arrangement by which all tips are pooled and divided among the staff, but the host cannot be sure of this and, in any case, it would be reasonable to give a separate tip of 2/6 to the waiter who has done the serving. In addition, it is customary to tip the wine waiter, that is, if he is not the person whom you have already paid for the meal. Other likely financial obligations are small tips (6d. or 1/-) for the cloakroom attendant and for the porter at the door if he gets you a taxi.

This 10% rule is of fairly wide application, but when

the bill is small it is usual to give more. For instance, if two people have coffee in the lounge of a hotel and the bill is 2/6, it would be reasonable to give the waiter 6d., not 3d. The same is true of tips to taxi drivers. In general, however, 10% is about right. To give less is ungenerous, unless the service has been very bad, while to give appreciably more, unless there are special reasons for it, is ostentatious, and unfair to other patrons of the establishment who abide by the normal rule.

At Theatres and Cinemas, etc.

There are one or two points for a host to remember on these occasions. Firstly, as the host, he will have the tickets, having either bought or booked them in advance. It is therefore correct for him to precede his guests, whether women or men, into the auditorium, so that he can hand the tickets to the attendant and have himself and his guests conducted to their seats. Secondly, he ought to decide beforehand the order in which the members of his party are to sit. There are no particular rules of precedence about this, but if his guests hesitate he should take charge to avoid holding up the passage of other patrons in the aisles, and the awkwardness of having to change places in the narrow space between one row and the next, to the inconvenience of people already seated. Thirdly, every effort should be made to get there before the play has begun. In a cinema where the programme is continuous late arrival does not greatly matter, though it is obviously better to take one's seat before the beginning of the picture than in the middle of it.

Punctuality.—In the theatre, on the other hand, punctuality is the politeness not only of princes but of lesser patrons. Nothing is more infuriating to those who have taken the trouble to arrive in time than to have late arrivals blundering past them in the dark and treading on toes as they grope their way to their seats. Besides it is maddening for the actors who are seeking to establish that "mutual contagion between stage and auditorium," as Sir Cedric Hardwicke put it, which is so essential in the theatre. Punctuality is likewise necessary at a concert. Again, if a party of five or six people go to the theatre, the host should buy two or three programmes, not merely one. Lastly—it is necessary to say this, though it ought not to be—members of the audience, whether they are hosts or guests, should not talk or whisper during the performance or rustle noisily in boxes of chocolates. Whether the increase of this pernicious habit is due to people watching television plays in their own homes, where they do not need to consider the feelings of others, or whether we should put it down to plain stupidity and rank bad manners is uncertain. The fact remains that people who ought to know better are often guilty of it, and thereby effectually spoil the pleasure of the majority of playgoers who want to surrender themselves to the illusion of the theatre.

Bad Manners in the Theatre.—When people offend in this way, a glance in their direction will sometimes indicate that their talking, rustling and whispering are unwelcome. If this has no effect, anyone sitting near is entitled to ask them to keep quiet. But any such request should be made politely: e.g. "Would you mind not talking, please? We can't hear what the actors are saying." However annoying interruptions may be it is a mistake to lose one's temper, for the rudeness of others does not excuse bad manners in oneself. Moreover, a

polite request may be more effective than a curt one. If
this proves unavailing, there is little that the victims of
bad behaviour can do except to wait until the interval
and then ask the attendant whether they can move into
seats in some other part of the house. As a last resort
complaint can be made to the manager. This may solve
the immediate problem, but the real solution continues
to lie in consideration on the part of everyone for the
feelings, rights and convenience of other people.

Leaving the Theatre.—Unless there is good reason, such
as the need to catch the last train home, people ought not
to leave a theatre or a concert hall until the performance
has finished. If they are obliged to leave, they should do
so as unobtrusively as possible. At the end of the performance there is still no justification for scrambling for
the exit doors as though the building were on fire. The
playing of the National Anthem may strike some people
as a meaningless formality, but that is no reason for
walking out in the middle of it. Nor is it unreasonable to

give the actors or the orchestra their meed of applause before making a move.

Etiquette Out of Doors

This chapter has been chiefly concerned with entertaining away from one's home. Since this process necessarily involves going out of doors to reach the place of entertainment, we may conveniently include here some observations about general behaviour and etiquette when meeting or accompanying people out of doors.

Walking in the Streets.—Traffic is required by law to keep to the left. There is no law governing the movement of pedestrians in this respect, though a person walking in a road where there is no pavement is recommended to keep to the right in order that he may see a vehicle approaching him in time for both to take evasive action. On pavements it is customary to keep to the right, though in busy cities this is not always practicable. Anyway, when a man is walking along the pavement with a lady he should place himself on her left, that is, nearer to the kerb. If he is accompanying two ladies, it is still correct for him to be in this position and not between them. In a crowded street it may not be possible to walk three abreast all the way, so the man must be prepared to drop behind when necessary. This practice of the man being nearer to the pavement edge than the lady is a survival of polite custom from former times. In the old days roads were apt to be very muddy, so the man exposed himself, rather than his companion, to the mud thrown up by passing carts and coaches. He was likewise the recipient of household refuse thrown out of windows in the days when the upper stories of houses projected further over the street than the lower, the person nearest to the wall of the house, therefore, being the best protected.

Having crossed a road and changed direction a man may find himself on the right of the lady and so will have to move to her left. But the time to do this is on reaching the pavement after crossing the road. He can then take up his proper position quite easily and naturally without

scuttling from one side of the lady to the other like a scrum-half waiting for the ball to be heeled out to him. In crossing the road or moving through a crowd a man should not offer a lady his arm unless she is elderly and needs help or unless, of course, he is on such close terms with her that he would normally do so anyway.

Meeting Slight Acquaintances.—When a lady and a man who are only slightly acquainted meet each other in the street, it is for the lady to acknowledge his presence with a slight bow or smile. For him to do so would give the impression of forcing himself upon her, so he should only raise his hat in reply to and not in anticipation of her greeting. In the same way it would then be for the lady to stop and talk to him, if she wished to do so. If two slight acquaintances of the same sex encounter each other it is for the elder to acknowledge the presence of the younger and not vice-versa. A man seeing a lady approaching him on his left should, if possible, raise his hat with his right hand, but use his left if she is coming towards him on his right. The reason is that he can then turn his head and smile in her direction without having his face obscured by his arm.

These are, perhaps, counsels of perfection, for how often do we pass people and only recognise them when they have gone by! Again, if recognition is simultaneous, can a man possibly be sure that he has waited until the lady bowed before taking off his hat? And how can a man raise his hat when he has an umbrella in one hand, a parcel in the other, and a brief-case under his arm? Besides, very few of the younger generation ever wear a hat at all!

The answer to such questions is simple. No code of etiquette can do more than lay down general rules. These are not rigid, admitting of no exception. If they were, there would be nothing grotesque in W. S. Gilbert's poem about the two castaways, each of whom kept to his own half of the desert island where they were stranded because neither had been previously introduced to the other. One might as well argue that it would be highly improper for anyone but her husband to rescue a lady from her bedroom in a burning house. You cannot frame rules to cover every contingency. A person with good manners should be able to adapt himself to circumstances, for politeness consists very largely of consideration for others. Etiquette may, in general terms, decree that you should not speak to a person to whom you have not been introduced. But it would be ridiculous to take this as meaning that you should ignore a stranger who stops you in the street to ask the way. On the contrary, courtesy requires that you should give him all the help you can. In the same way, if you are bare-headed or have your

hands full so that you cannot take off your hat, you can nevertheless bow or smile at a passing acquaintance. You would give cause for offence only if you walked by without any sign of recognition. While we are on the subject of raising hats there is one point that needs to be emphasised. When two men pass each other in the street they may merely nod or wave a greeting, particularly if they know each other fairly well. But if one of them is accompanied by a lady, the other man must raise his hat and his friend should respond in the same way. This holds good whether the man walking by himself knows the lady or not.

Going by Taxi

When two people, a man and a woman, go by taxi, he will naturally open the door so that she may get in first. She should take her seat on the far side of the cab, so that he does not have to push past her in order to sit

down himself. When the taxi reaches its destination the man is expected to get out first so that he may help his companion to alight. This is easy enough if the cab pulls up with the male passenger in the same position relative to the pavement as he was when he got in. But if the cab has halted on the other side of the road etiquette may have to give way to road safety. Either the man must push past the lady or he must open the door on his own side, which in crowded streets is often far from safe, and walk round behind the taxi to the pavement. In these circumstances it is probably best to let the lady get out first.

Paying Taxi Fares.—When leaving a dance or a theatre after a performance there may be some difficulty in getting a taxi, especially on a wet night. In such a case it would be perfectly correct and indeed considerate for a man to offer to share a taxi with other people even though they are strangers to him. It would be for these others to accept if the destination of both parties is in the same direction, to decline if it is not. If the offer is accepted the man who gets out first should insist on paying his share of the fare, as it would be inconsiderate to repay an act of courtesy on the part of a stranger by saddling him with additional expense. On his side, the other man should accept the offer, appreciating that his fleeting companion would find it embarrassing to be under a financial obligation to someone he does not know. The best method of achieving the desired result is for the one who gets out first to thank the other for his courtesy and to pay the taxi-driver himself for the journey up to that point, instead of handing a few shillings to the man still in the cab.

Paying for Oneself

When a man invites someone else to be his guest at dinner or at a theatre he, as host, assumes responsibility for paying all expenses, including such incidental expenses as tips and taxi-fares. His guest is at liberty to offer to pay a share of such extras, but it would, in fact, be ungracious for the guest to press the point and for the host to accept the offer.

There are many occasions, however, when sharing expenses is proper and reasonable. Nowadays a very large number of women are earning their own living and therefore take the view that they should bear their share of the expenses involved in going out to dinner or to a play. When the two persons concerned are of the same sex and of similar age or standing an equal division of expenses between the two is quite usual. Alternatively, if one acts as host on one occasion the other will assume the rôle next time, which comes to the same thing. That is simple enough. With a man and a girl, on the other hand, care may be needed on both sides. No difficulty is likely to arise when the pair have known each other for a long time or when the relations between them are firmly established on a purely friendly basis. In such circumstances the girl can readily make it clear that, for instance, she wants to go to a certain dance and would like him to take her, but on the understanding that it is to be a 'Dutch treat,' and that she will pay her share of the expenses.

When a man, having met a girl a few times in the company of other friends, invites her out to dinner or to come to a dance with him, the reason, surely, is that he finds her attractive and would like to know her better. If this feeling is not reciprocated, the girl has only to decline this and subsequent invitations on the pretext of previous engagements. If, on the other hand, she is interested in him, she will doubtless accept the invitation and go as his guest. If he did not want her company he would not have asked her. After one or two such outings, the girl can raise the question of paying her own share in future. By this time she should know something about him and be able to say in effect: "I enjoy going out with you. I should like to do it again. But I'm earning my living, you're not a millionaire, and it's not fair that you should go on paying for both of us every time. So either I must stop going with you, which would be a pity, or

you must let me pay my share." She may be the more
inclined to express this point of view if she suspects that
his feelings towards her are warmer than those she has
for him. She can then, as it were, detach herself or stabilise
the position on a firm basis of friendship without giving
him any grounds for feeling that she has led him on or
shown herself to be a 'gold-digger'. It is not within the
scope of this book to give hints about the handling of such
situations. The point here is simply that there is no reason
at all why a girl should not pay her own share of expenses
on occasions, but she should bear in mind that it may
give a man real pleasure to take her out. Therefore if she
wants to pay her own expenses she must make this
plain to begin with, and not suddenly raise the matter
when the waiter presents the bill. Once again, it is a
question of consideration for the feelings of someone
else.

Giving Up One's Seat in a Bus

Not so long ago the most elementary sense of good
manners caused a man to offer his seat in a bus or tram
to any lady who would otherwise have had to stand.
Children, too, were brought up to give up their seats for
a lady and often for an elderly man. Latterly there has
been a marked change. In part this is due to a general
lowering in the standard of politeness in the post-war
world. In the main it is the outcome of changes in the
status of women. There is now a much greater degree of
equality between the sexes. Women now enjoy the
same political rights as men, and have thereby in the
opinion of many men forfeited any claim to preferential
treatment in other matters. Consequently a man returning
home at the end of a day's work may feel under no

obligation to give up his seat to a woman whether she has a paid job or is a housewife.

Under these changed conditions it is difficult to lay down rigid rules, particularly when, if a man does give up his seat, a woman may take it without bothering to thank him. Yet there is no justification for being impolite merely because other people are. Perhaps the best solution is for a man to offer his seat to an elderly woman, to a mother with a child in her arms and to any person of either sex who is obviously infirm. It is probable that a man would also give up his seat in favour of a good-looking woman. There is no reason why he should not, but in such a case he does so less from politeness than because it gives him pleasure. He cannot expect thereby to acquire merit!

CHAPTER VI

TRAVEL

Staying at Hotels

Anyone proposing to stay at a hotel should, whenever possible, write or telephone to book accommodation. When the manager informs him this is available the visitor should accept it by letter. Hotel proprietors cannot be expected to keep an offer open indefinitely and, unless the visitor has confirmed the reservation, he has only himself to blame if he finds on arrival that the rooms are already occupied by other people. For a stay of more than one night he should ascertain in advance the cost of room and board. If he wishes to go to a holiday resort and has no knowledge of the hotels there, he may be able to get information by writing to the office of the Town Clerk. If he intends to travel by car and is a member of the Automobile Association, he can obtain from the Head Office details of the route he should take from his starting point to his destination.

Signing the Register.—Proprietors of hotels and boarding-houses are required to keep a list of all those who stay overnight in their establishments.

A man travelling by himself and having no title or service rank should put his normal signature: e.g. "R. H. Adair" or "Robin Adair." A lady travelling by herself should indicate whether she is married or single: e.g. "Mrs. H. Sutherland"; "Miss G. Sharp." A husband accompanied by his wife would put, say: "Mr. and Mrs. Holmes." If a grown up daughter was with them, he would add: "Miss Holmes." If the couple have two small children with them the husband need not give their names, but may add to the entry of his wife and himself the words: "and family." A man with a title or service rank should indicate this whether he is travelling alone or not: e.g. "Colonel H. Jackson," "Sir George and Lady Castle," "Dr. and Mrs. McTaggart." But the entry: "Mr. G. Smith" is incorrect. It should be: "G. Smith," or "George Smith."

Behaviour in a Hotel

The old saying about an Englishman's home being his castle is in these bureaucratic days a good deal less true than it may once have been. But it still implies that, provided he does not break local bye-laws or annoy the neighbours by turning on his wireless set too loudly, he may do more or less as he pleases within the privacy of his own home. In a hotel, on the other hand, he has to consider other people besides himself and his family. All the guests have as much right as he to the amenities that the place provides. Consequently he must not monopolise a bathroom for long periods, talk loudly to his friends in one of the public rooms when other guests are reading or obviously want to listen to the wireless, nor should he walk noisily along corridors or disturb the rest of other people by banging about in his bedroom if he goes to bed late. If a couple have young children with them, they should do their best to keep them quiet in the public rooms. There is no need to prolong this list of injunctions. They and others like them provide a sufficient reminder that just because a guest has paid for his rooms he is not thereby entitled to be rowdy or inconsiderate. The other guests have likewise paid, and it behoves him to show as much consideration for them as they should do for him.

Behaviour to Fellow Guests.—In general it is in ordinary circumstances incorrect to speak to someone without an introduction. In a small private hotel or guest-house, particularly one in which people stay for long periods, as many elderly people do nowadays, the manageress will sometimes make a new-comer known to the other semi-permanent residents. In larger hotels people stay for a few weeks at most and often only for a night or two. In such circumstances, not only is there as a rule no one to effect introductions, but even if there were it would not be proper for him to do so. The fact that people happen by chance to find themselves under the roof of the same hotel does not constitute a reason why they should be expected, much less compelled, to strike up an acquaintance with other temporary visitors. Equally, however, there is no justification for one group of guests to act as though the others did not exist. There is a courteous middle course between aloofness on the one hand and undue familiarity on the other.

Thus, on the morrow of his arrival at a hotel, a new-comer, entering the dining-room, for instance, should be prepared to say: "Good morning", as he takes his place, to guests at adjacent tables, or to make some comment on that safe but inexhaustible topic, the weather, to the person occupied like himself in gloomy contemplation of the barometer in the entrance hall. In other words, he should be ready to acknowledge the presence of others without intruding on their privacy, to move his chair so that another can share the warmth of the fire, to make way for a lady on the stairs, and so on.

It is easy for a married couple or a family party to

strike the correct note in their dealings with fellow guests in a hotel, because they constitute, as it were, a self-contained little group and have only to observe the small courtesies indicated above. It is rather more difficult for a single person, particularly for a youngish woman. A man can make a few trivial remarks to a guest of his own sex or pass the time of day with a lady in the lounge of a hotel. At the worst he will lay himself open to the charge of being a bore, and to that only if he prolongs his observations when his neighbour is trying to read the paper. A lady, unaccompanied, may have to be more circumspect since she must not give the impression of trying to scrape an acquaintance with members of the opposite sex.

After a day or two it is civil to mention one's name to a guest with whom one has reached the stage of falling into casual conversation in the lounge. But it is particularly important not to be snobbish or patronising by dragging into the conversation prominent people whom one may happen to know. On the whole it is best to confine the talk to general topics.

Complaints.—Nowadays many hotels in this country have difficulty in providing adequate staff. Allowances should be made for this, but it may nevertheless happen that a guest will have legitimate grounds for complaint about perfunctory service, unsatisfactory meals and the like. It is, however, extremely ill-bred for a guest to voice his complaint in public, still more so for him to abuse the waiter. For one thing, the man himself may not be responsible in any way for whatever has led to the complaint. For another, it is highly embarrassing for the other guests to have to listen to an argument which has nothing to do with them, but which they are unable to avoid overhearing. The correct procedure is for the guest to go quietly to the manager's office and draw his attention to what has happened.

Visiting a Friend at a Hotel.—We have seen that when someone entertains guests at a restaurant it is his duty to be on the spot in time to receive them. In the same way if someone staying in a hotel is expecting a friend to call, or has invited one to a meal, he should be waiting, if possible, in the lounge for the visitor to arrive. Should a visitor thus invited fail to find his friend in the lounge, he should go to the reception desk of the hotel, give his name, and ask the clerk to telephone to the person's room to say that Mr. X has arrived. He should not himself go up to the room unless the occupant when answering the telephone tells the clerk to ask him to do so. For obvious reasons, a girl staying in a hotel should not invite a man friend up to her room, but rather ask the clerk to inform her visitor that she will come down in a few minutes.

Tipping in Hotels.—Hotel managers will not usually accept cheques in payment of accounts unless the guest has stayed at the hotel before. When asking for his bill a guest should enquire whether a charge for service is included in it. If it is, there is no need for him to tip the chambermaid or dining-room staff, unless he particularly wishes to, and even then the amount should be small. But it is usual, even where service is included, to give a small tip to the hall porter who brings down your luggage and puts it into a taxi or into your car. If no fixed charge for service is added to the bill, the general rule that tips should amount to about 10% of it holds good, the major portion being given to the waiter, and rather less to the chambermaid. A guest who has spent only one night at a hotel will probably find that a reasonable tip will come to rather more than the 10% which is proper for a stay of a week or more. If the bill for dinner, bed and breakfast comes to, say, 30/-, it is difficult to divide 3/- among several members of the staff without being niggardly, whereas £1 for a week's stay at a ten guinea a week hotel will, with the possible addition of a shilling or two, do well enough. At a luxury hotel, again, some addition to the normal percentage may be necessary, if only because the various functionaries are apt to be so imposing and resplendent that few people are sufficiently unintimidated to adhere to a strict 10%. Besides, at such places, a number of the guests are liable to be inordinately rich, so that one must either accept the prevailing rate— or, preferably, stay elsewhere.

Travelling Abroad

The Importance of Good Behaviour.—During the period of prohibition in the United States the unrestrained drinking in which some of the citizens of that country indulged when touring Europe and elsewhere did, for the time being, a great deal of harm to the good name of their native land in the eyes of foreigners with whom such visitors came in contact. In the same way the scanty clothing and unseemly behaviour of some passengers on Mediterranean cruises produced an unfavourable impression of the British in some of the coastal towns at which the vessels put in.

Clearly anyone sufficiently mindful of etiquette and good behaviour to read a book such as this will not comport himself in a reprehensible fashion. These two examples are therefore given only to emphasize the fact that anyone travelling abroad is not only a single unimportant individual. He is representative, in however small a way, of his country, and is liable to be regarded as such by the peoples of other lands in which he travels. Our opinion of foreign countries is often governed less by international events than by the impression made on us by individual foreigners whom we happen to meet. For this reason, as well as for their own self-respect, people ought to behave abroad not worse, but if anything, better than they are accustomed to do at home.

National Customs.—The principles that govern good manners are much the same in any country, but every nation has its own customs. In England, for instance, there is no need to tip the attendant who shows you to your seat in a theatre. It is a common occurrence to hear tourists on their return from a trip to Paris complaining that they were forced to tip the attendant at the *Comédie Française* or (more often) the *Folies Bergère*. There is no denying, of course, that especially in some countries and in places frequented by tourists there is a tendency on the part of some of the local inhabitants to exploit the foreign visitor. But in the particular case just mentioned there was no such attempt for, whereas in England a theatre attendant receives a weekly wage, her French counterpart is paid either nothing or very little, and is therefore authorised to levy toll on the theatre patrons whom she shows to their seats. Sometimes a tourist cannot be expected to know that he is infringing the local code of politeness and, as a rule, the inhabitants of the country, realising this, will make allowances for it. Again, an example from theatre-going will serve. In this country when we have to pass other people in order to reach our seats in the middle of a row, we invariably face the stage as we move towards our places. But in Sweden it is considered extremely rude to present, in the architectural phrase, one's "south aspect" to the people whom one passes. The correct procedure is to face the people in the row, not the stage.

In England people shake hands with a new acquaintance when they are being introduced, and with their host and hostess when they greet or take leave of them at a party. In some countries, France, for example, handshakes are exchanged not only on such, but on almost all occasions. A man who meets a few friends at a café will shake hands with all of them, even though he may see them every day. This may strike us as unnecessary, even fulsome, but the British visitor meeting French acquaintances abroad should comply with the custom of the country. Moreover, if he meets a lady in the street, he should raise his hat without waiting for her to bow to him. Again, in a restaurant, in a public room or the lift of a hotel, he should take off his hat in any foreign country (and, for that matter, at home). This applies to everybody, except possibly to American detectives who, to judge from the films, have a rooted objection to removing their hats under any circumstances.

In some restaurants in the United Kingdom, fortunately not all, the customer has the impression of being regarded as a necessary evil to be fed and got rid of as soon as possible. In restaurants abroad, on the other hand, he is more likely to be made welcome. It is important, therefore, that the tourist should acknowledge with a smile the presence of the manager or waiter who comes forward, and not brush unceremoniously past him to sit down morosely at the nearest vacant table.

All these are perhaps minor matters. No tourist, least of all one visiting a country for the first time, can be

EGM—D*

familiar with local social usage. He can take comfort from the thought that unwitting breaches of etiquette will readily be overlooked, provided that his general conduct conforms with the normal universal rules of good manners. A pleasant demeanour and kindly intentions will atone for ignorance on points of detail. Arrogance is an unendearing trait, and anybody who shows by his manner that he thinks himself superior to "a lot of foreigners" will get little or nothing out of a holiday abroad, and quite possibly do a good deal of harm. Tourists may be forgiven for not knowing any language but their own, though they will enjoy themselves a great deal more if they take the trouble to learn a few words of the language of the country they propose to visit. What is unpardonable is for a tourist to assume that foreigners are necessarily as ignorant as himself and that, if he loudly disparages the ways of their country, none of them will understand or resent his remarks. Yet the offender would be the first to wax indignant if he heard a foreigner running down Britain in the same way.

Letters of Introduction

When someone moves to another neighbourhood or pays an extended visit to another country, it is not uncommon for him to present letters of introduction to people already living in the place he plans to visit, so that he may get to know them and, through their good offices, other people as well. It frequently happens also that a man with an interest in some particular subject will be put in touch with another with similar tastes or aptitudes through a third party. If this third person has little or no acquaintance with the man who has sought his help, or if the matter is a purely business or professional one, he will possibly do no more than take one of his visiting cards and write at the top of it: "To introduce Mr. George Stevens." Mr. Stevens (or whoever he may be) will then go to the home or office of the person he is anxious to see and present the card. The recipient, knowing the man by whom the stranger is introduced, can then either see him immediately or else fix a time for him to call. The fact that his friend has done no more than write a few words on a card indicates that the writer has no great personal knowledge of the man he is thus introducing.

Writing Letters of Introduction.—Anybody who undertakes to write a letter of introduction has a certain responsibility. There is an old saying to the effect that, though we are given our relatives, we can at least choose our own friends. The recipient of a letter of introduction is denied this freedom of choice, because courtesy demands that he should add to his own circle of friends or acquaintances a person introduced into it by someone else.

It is difficult to ask for a letter of introduction, and no request for one should be made unless the seeker of this favour knows the prospective writer fairly well, and has no reason to suppose that he would be reluctant to grant it. It is therefore more satisfactory when a person, knowing that such a letter would be helpful, offers to write one without being asked. But before surrendering to this generous impulse he ought to consider whether the stranger is likely to prove a congenial acquaintance or not, for it is unfair out of a mistaken sense of kindness to one person to lay an unwelcome burden on the shoulders of another.

The Form of such Letters.—Letters of Introduction

should be short and should not include irrelevant topics. The envelope containing the letter should be addressed to the recipient, but the flap should not be stuck down. If it were, the person who is to present it might jump to the conclusion that the writer has made statements about him which he does not want him to read. It is essential, therefore, that he should be able to satisfy himself of the contents of the letter, should he wish to do so. Indeed, the writer will often show him the letter before putting it in the envelope, with the words: "You may care to see what I have said. I hope you think it will do," or something of the kind. If he does not do this, the envelope is, after all, open in case the bearer wishes to read it. Etiquette probably prescribes that he should refrain from doing so, though curiosity will doubtless prove stronger in this instance than etiquette. Either way no harm is done.

Specimen Letters of Introduction.—(*a*) When the writer is prepared to vouch for the person concerned but has little personal knowledge of him or, in this case, her.

> 14, Lennox Gardens,
> Scarborough,
> 17th April, 19—

My dear Mary,

With the bearer of this letter, Miss Stebbing, I am myself only slightly acquainted, but she is the niece of Hilda Scott, one of my oldest friends, of whom I have often spoken to you. Violet Stebbing is shortly going to Geneva to take up a secretarial job with the World Health Organisation. At present she knows nobody there and it would, I am sure, be a great comfort to Hilda to feel that there was someone in Geneva who could keep a friendly eye on her niece, and perhaps help her to get to know people. She would therefore be very grateful for anything you can do—and so should I.

Yours affectionately,
Jane.

(b) When the writer is a friend of the person on whose behalf he is writing.

18, Mount Road,
York.

5th September, 19—

Dear Crawford,

It gives me great pleasure to introduce to you Henry Trench, the bearer of this letter. I have known him for many years, particularly since the end of the War when we moved into the house next door to his. He is shortly retiring and, for reasons of health, his wife's rather than his own, has been advised to settle in the South of England. When he told me recently that he proposed to stay for a few weeks in Eastbourne, while looking round for a house in the neighbourhood, I at once thought of putting him into touch with you. Like you, he is a keen gardener, and plays a good game of golf, so you will have tastes in common. I am sure I can count on you to make him and his wife feel at home in their new surroundings.

Yours ever,
John Harvey.

In both these letters the writer explains the reasons why she/he feels justified in making the bearer known, gives some information about the person's background and circumstances and, in the second case, some first-hand information about his tastes.

Presenting a Letter of Introduction.—If the letter (or card) of introduction has been written for a business or professional as opposed to a social purpose, the bearer will doubtless present it in person, and the recipient can ask his visitor to sit down while he reads it. A social letter of introduction should, however, be sent with a brief note or visiting card attached to it, indicating the address at which the bearer can be reached.

Acknowledging a Letter of Introduction.—This should be done as promptly as possible, since to take no notice of it for some time could reasonably be considered by the bearer of it as a slight, if not a positive snub. The recipient should therefore write or telephone within a day or so of receiving the letter, and invite the newcomer to, say, lunch or tea. Alternatively, a call should be made at the hotel or other address at which the bearer is to be found. From that point onwards the acquaintance thus begun may develop or languish according to the feelings of the parties concerned. If they take to one another friendship will follow naturally. If the recipient does not find the newcomer congenial he should, nevertheless, if only to please the friend who had written, make him welcome. Duty thus done he can with a clear conscience, see less and less of him as time goes on. On the other hand, the newcomer may prove to be a permanent asset.

One word of warning remains to be said. It is no kindness to write a letter of introduction to foreign friends when the person introduced knows no language but his own and the foreigners can speak no English. They will find it incumbent upon them to invite the newcomer to their home only to find that neither he nor they can converse in any common tongue. The ensuing ordeal is likely to be agonising for all concerned. But the real culprit is the person who wrote the letter without making it clear that the bearer was no linguist.

Newcomers to a Place

Newcomers settling in a place strange to them sometimes find it difficult to get to know people, particularly if they have retired and therefore do not have the opportunity to make acquaintances at their place of work or business. The initiative in breaking the social ice used formerly to rest with the old-established residents who, after making discreet enquiries, would decide whether to call upon the newcomers or not. If they decided against doing so the position of the new arrivals was apt to be forlorn. Nowadays, when few people have much time or money for entertaining and the practice of calling has largely died out, this rather arbitrary method of dealing with newcomers no longer applies.

What then are such new arrivals to do? As mentioned previously, letters of introduction may provide a solution. If they have none, a useful practical step, which they may take without fear of rebuff, is for them to leave a note at the vicarage or rectory of the nearest parish church, explaining that they have recently come to live in the place and asking the clergyman to call on them. This they may do even if they are not regular church-goers. When the clergyman comes to visit them, they can tell him that they would like to get to know some people and ask for his help. This will be the more easy for them if, without thrusting themselves forward, they express their readiness to participate in the social activities of the parish, and to contribute something to the life of the place in which they have come to live.

CHAPTER VII

GETTING ENGAGED

Parental Influence

"Pardon me," said the redoubtable Lady Bracknell to her daughter, "you are not engaged to anyone. When you do become engaged to someone, I or your father, should his health permit him, will inform you of the fact. An engagement should come on a young girl as a surprise, pleasant or unpleasant as the case may be. It is hardly a matter that she should be allowed to arrange for herself."

Oscar Wilde was caricaturing rather than portraying real life in *The Importance of Being Earnest*. Jane Austen, writing a century earlier, depicted the contemporary scene with a good deal of accuracy as well as quiet humour, and any reader of her novels will recall the importance attached by anxious mothers to the social and financial position of a potential son-in-law. Again, is it not widely believed that in France marriages are arranged between two sets of parents with little regard to the feelings of the son and daughter concerned? It would be much nearer the mark to say that the French, a practical people in such matters, take the view that a marriage is more likely to be successful when the partners to it have the same sort of social background and upbringing, tastes in common and roughly comparable financial resources.

But however large the degree of parental intervention or influence may have been at different periods, the position as the result of two World Wars and consequent social changes, is very different from what it once was. A modern Lady Bracknell rather than her daughter might now be the one to be surprised by the news of the latter's engagement.

Young people, no doubt, must always have resented attempts to hamper their freedom of action in a matter so vitally affecting their happiness. Under present conditions when many girls are earning their own living, they would be even less ready than formerly to yield to parental influence. Yet in the more liberal conditions of today something like 30,000 marriages are ended in the divorce courts every year, which suggests that greater freedom of choice does not of itself guarantee a successful marriage. One of Somerset Maugham's characters stated that the only way a woman could find out whether or not she was in love with a man was to ask herself if she could use his toothbrush! A cynical observation, perhaps, but a necessary reminder that marriage is a matter of prosaic breakfasts on Monday mornings as well as of romantic dinners on Saturday nights. In short, while love at first sight is perfectly possible and may prove enduring, it is generally wiser, so far as circumstance and temperament allow, to take a little time before deciding to get engaged.

Consideration for Parents

In the old days a prospective suitor was required to seek out a girl's parents and ask their permission to pay his addresses to her. This is no longer essential, and to do so would now be the exception rather than the rule. Often, indeed, the parents of a girl earning her own living away from home and perhaps writing to them seldom may not be aware that their daughter is acquainted with a young man, much less thinking of becoming engaged to him.

Assuming that such a young couple are both twenty-one years old or more, it is unlikely that there could be any legal objection to their getting married, but for them to do so without the knowledge, let alone the approval of their parents would certainly be wrong, unless the circumstances were altogether exceptional.

Etiquette, as has already been emphasised, is concerned with correct procedure. But it is not merely a matter of rules. It rests firmly on a basis of good manners and consideration for others. Very often, of course, two sets of parents who are old friends or near neighbours will not be astonished to discover that the son of one pair and the daughter of the other want to get married. They have seen the friendship ripen. But if the young man is almost a stranger to the girl's parents, it would be in the highest degree inconsiderate on the part of the young couple if an announcement of their engagement in the paper were to be the first intimation that one or both sets of parents had of how matters stood between them.

Breaking the News

When the two families know each other the procedure is simple. The young man, having proposed to the girl and been accepted, has only to go, probably taking her with him, to break the news, which may come as no surprise, to her parents and to his own. But if the man has little or no acquaintance with the parents of the girl to whom he has proposed, he should take the earliest opportunity of going to see them. Legally, it may not be necessary for him to ask their consent. He should try, nevertheless, to put himself in their place and to realize their natural anxiety and concern for their daughter's welfare. The girl herself would normally be eager to introduce him to her parents. Even if, for some reason, she was on bad terms with them, it would still be her duty to bring him to see them.

The same would be true if she had met her fiancé while travelling abroad and for that reason had not previously had the opportunity of making him known to her parents. The young man, for his part, should be prepared to give his future parents-in-law information about himself, his family, his work, his prospects and so on. Moreover, especially if the girl is very young and he is a comparative stranger to her parents, he should not think it unreasonable if they were to favour a long, rather than a short, engagement, in order that they might get to know him better. People take each other in marriage for better or worse, but unless they are fundamentally selfish, they have also to endeavour to make the best of their new relations. In short, they ought to show them consideration, an attitude likewise required of the parents themselves.

When all the parties know each other well little adjustment to the new situation is needed. But it is obvious that, when one of the engaged couple is a virtual stranger to the other's parents, or when the two sets of parents know each other little or not at all, the situation calls for tact and good sense.

Announcing the Engagement

No public announcement of an engagement should be made until both sets of parents have been informed of the couple's intention to get married. If the respective parents do not yet know one another, it would normally rest with the parents of the man to write to the girl and to her mother to arrange an early meeting. It may be that the parents on one side feel some misgivings about the proposed marriage. In that case they can legitimately suggest that no date should be fixed for the wedding for the time being, or perhaps that the engagement should be regarded as unofficial. But they ought not to go further whatever their own private feelings may be. The engaged couple presumably know their own minds, and actively to oppose the match would not only be undignified but very possibly lead to estrangement.

In most cases, no doubt, the parents on either side would signify approval, and the next step would be for the bride and her mother to inform near relatives and close friends of the engagement either by letter or by word of mouth. The fiancé would do likewise with his own intimate circle. Not until this has been done should the engagement be made known in the papers. The bride's mother usually inserts and pays for the announcement, because the wedding arrangements are in the main the responsibility of the bride's rather than of the bridegroom's family. Whether the notice appears in *The Daily Telegraph* and *The Times* or in a local paper, it will take the same form. The following imaginary examples will serve:—

1. Lieutenant R. J. Roseveare, R.N. and Miss S. H. Greaves.

   "The engagement is announced between Lieutenant Robert James Roseveare, R.N., younger son of Mr. and Mrs. Richard Roseveare, of Farnborough House, Guildford, Surrey, and Susan Helen, only daughter of Mr. and Mrs. Raymond Greaves of The Point, Brixham, Devonshire."

2. Mr. R. Cotswold and Miss D. M. Evans.

   "The engagement is announced between Robert,

only surviving son of the late Major F. H. Cotswold and of Mrs. Cotswold of 476, Chelsea Walk, S.W.3., and Denise Marion, eldest daughter of Mr. and Mrs. Donald Evans of Copse Farm, Henfield, Sussex."

3. Mr. R. S. Lumsden and Miss G. A. Farley.

"A marriage has been arranged and will shortly take place between Roderick Sanders, son of Major George Lumsden of Wickham Court, Tavistock, and of Mrs. L. Templeton of 57, Marlborough Rd., Hatfield, and Georgina Anne, elder daughter of Sir George and Lady Farley of Oxburgh House, Taunton, Somerset."

Note.—(*a*) The surnames of the engaged couple are usually omitted in the announcements, as in examples 2 and 3. But there is no definite rule (see Example 1).

(*b*) In the third example the implication is that the parents of the bridegroom are divorced, and that the mother has now remarried. When the parents are not divorced but living apart, this can be indicated by putting . . . "elder son of Col. R. H. —— of 9, The Parade, Leominster and of Mrs. —— of Sittingbourne, Kent."

(*c*) Newspapers always state, usually at the head or foot of the appropriate column, the rates they charge for notices of births, engagements, marriages and deaths. It is important that a cheque should be enclosed with the text of the announcement, for without it the insertion may be delayed. It is easy to estimate the approximate cost of such an announcement by comparing the length of the proposed one with that of others already to be found in some issue of the paper concerned.

The Engagement Ring

As soon as a man has been accepted by the girl of his

choice he should buy an engagement ring, and put it on the third finger of her left hand.

In romantic novels the hero sometimes produces a ring from his pocket immediately after proposing. In real life this practice is not to be encouraged. For one thing, it

suggests a certain cocksureness on the part of the suitor, which is not flattering to his fiancée. For another, a ring purchased in advance may not fit! The pair should rather go together to a jeweller's shop, where the girl may choose for herself. The young man will naturally wish to be generous, but unless she knows him to be very well off, his fiancée, while choosing a ring that she likes, should give some consideration to the price.

Length of the Engagement

There are no hard and fast rules about the length of an engagement. But, in general, a fairly short one is to be preferred. In some ways, of course, it is a rapturous period, but it is also tantalising and unsettling. Sometimes the length of an engagement is determined by circumstances. The prospective bridegroom, for example, may be a medical student who will be in no position to support himself, much less a wife, until after he has passed his final examinations. Again, if the fiancée is very young, her parents may urge delay in order to give her time to make quite sure that she knows her own mind. When for financial or other reasons marriage is likely to be postponed for a year or more, it is probably better not to announce the engagement at all, but to allow the couple to be unofficially engaged, only near relatives and close friends being informed of it. When force of circumstances does not impose a particular period of time, it is usual for an engagement to be a matter of a few months.

Breaking off an Engagement

From time to time one comes across a laconic statement at the foot of a series of notices of engagements in the paper. It runs:— "The marriage arranged between Mr. — and Miss — will not take place."

Friends of the couple concerned should copy the reticence of this announcement and not enquire into the causes which led up to its insertion. It is painful enough to break off an engagement. To put up with inquisitive questions from other people on the subject would be intolerable. No doubt those most closely connected with the pair will know what lies behind the announcement, but other people should not pry into the affair. They have no right to ask for explanations and if, for some reason, a couple decide that they are not after all well suited to one another, it is surely better to discover this before rather than after marriage. The girl will, of course, return the ring to her ex-fiancé and also give back to their donors any wedding presents which she may already have received.

Announcement of the Date of a Wedding

The first notice in the paper announces the engagement and may (as in example 3 on p. 117) indicate that the marriage will take place soon. Sometimes it may be found convenient to insert a second notice stating the place, date and time of the wedding. The customary wording would be as follows:—

Mr. F. R. Fortescue and Miss Somersham.

"The marriage of Mr. F. R. Fortescue, of Lower Beeding Hall, Sussex, with Olivia Mary, daughter of Mr. and Mrs. Neil Somersham, of Dryburgh House, Brighton, will take place at 2.30 p.m. on Wednesday, 25th May, at St. Mary Magdalen's Church, Hove."

A notice of this kind is not often necessary. The first one has made the engagement public and the particulars contained in the second can, as a rule, more conveniently be conveyed in the formal wedding invitation sent to individual relatives and friends.

Choosing Wedding Presents

The prospective bride will doubtless inform close friends and relatives by letter or by word of mouth of the date of her wedding. Others may not know it until they have received an invitation to the ceremony. But as soon as by one or other of these means the guests do know when the wedding is to take place, it is time for them to think about sending a wedding present.

Near relations should have no great difficulty in deciding what to give. Being relatives they can ask the prospective recipient what he or she would like. Very close friends can doubtless do the same, and are therefore in no need of advice on this matter.

For others the choice may be less simple. In these days when the housing problem is acute many newly-married couples may have at first to live with relations or perhaps in furnished rooms. For them a cheque would often be the most welcome form of present, since it can be paid into the bank and the money kept until the couple set up house on their own.

Even if the couple will begin their married life in a house or flat of their own, a cheque may still be an acceptable present, since the bride can use the money to buy something that she needs for the home. Sometimes people of moderate means shrink from giving a present in this form because, while the cost, say, of a salad bowl is not known except to the purchaser, the amount of a cheque is not in doubt. But there is no need for them to feel diffident or embarrassed. A cheque sent as a wedding present can be for any sum, from a guinea or two upwards. Moreover, if at the wedding reception the presents are displayed, the amount of a cheque is not disclosed any more than is the price paid for, say, a set of cocktail glasses. The names of people who gave cheques should be set down in a list which is on view with the other presents, but there is no mention of the amount of any cheque.

Many people feel, however, that a cheque, though welcome, is a drab and unimaginative kind of present, and consequently prefer to give something else. There are many things that a newly married couple will be glad to have more than one of. But there is a strict limit to the number of toast-racks, fire-irons or hat-stands that a couple can do with. It is better therefore to choose things such as tea-services, table-cloths, knives and forks, of which it is difficult to have too many. Some duplication is almost inevitable, but this can be much reduced if the mother of the bride keeps a list of a wide variety of things, from ashtrays to dining-room chairs, which she knows her daughter would like. On being consulted by friends she can suggest items from her list, mentioning the less expensive to people whose means she knows to be modest. In this way she can ensure, at least to some extent, that duplication is avoided, and at the same time help people to choose something within the means of the purchaser and really welcome to the recipient.

Acknowledging Wedding Presents

This should be done as promptly as possible. No one will expect a long letter, since they will realize that the engaged couple, and particularly the bride, will have a great deal to do in preparing for the wedding. But any giver of a present has a right to receive an expression of appreciation and thanks. Therefore, as a practical step, the recipient should keep a list showing the name of the giver, the nature of the gift, the date of its coming and a final column for a tick to show that it has been acknowledged. This saves a good deal of trouble and reduces to a minimum the risk either of not acknowledging a present at all, or, which is worse, of thanking one person for a present given by someone else.

CHAPTER VIII

GETTING MARRIED

Choosing the Church

Although by no means everyone nowadays is a regular church-goer, most couples prefer to be married in church. While the wedding preparations are still in a very early stage it is necessary to decide where the ceremony is to take place. If the families of the groom and the bride both attend the same church or live in the same parish the decision is obvious. Should they live in different parishes it is customary, in the absence of any compelling reason to the contrary,[1] for the wedding to be held in the church where the bride and her family worship or, to put it another way, in the church of the parish in which they live.

Having decided on the church it is usual for the engaged couple to go and see the Rector or Vicar of it. To do so is not merely a courteous action but a necessary one, for it would be stupid to go ahead with the preparations or to have invitations printed without having first made sure that arrangements have not already been made for another wedding in the same church and at the same time.

If the couple already know the parson they can either speak to him at the end of a service they have attended, or call at the vicarage at an hour when they think he is

---

[1] If one of the engaged couple is a Roman Catholic, the wedding will be solemnised in a Roman Catholic church. Any children of the marriage will, moreover, be brought up in the Roman Catholic faith.

likely to be in. If they are not regular church-goers, it may be best for the future bridegroom to write and ask for an appointment. Such a letter might be worded as follows:—

The Rev.: M. Trubshaw,
St. Botolph's Vicarage,
Camberley.
Dear Sir,

I have not had the pleasure of meeting you but, as you may possibly have heard, I have recently had the good fortune to become engaged to Miss Mary Ellis who, although her work has taken her away a good deal lately, still makes her permanent home with her parents at 9, Hatchard Gardens. My fiancée and I intend to get married towards the end of May, and we should very much like the wedding to take place at St. Botolph's. I must confess that I am very vague about the necessary formalities, so it would be a great help to us if we could have a talk with you about arrangements. May I ask you therefore to suggest some time next week when it would be convenient for you to see us?

Yours very truly,
Roger Blake.

At the resultant meeting, and others which may follow, a number of points would need to be considered. In addition to the engaged couple, the mother of the bride, who will in practice be largely responsible for the arrangements, will very likely be present. It will be convenient here to set down some of the points for consideration.

Date and Time of Wedding.—A number of the guests whom it is proposed to invite may not be readily available in the middle of the week, so that for them a Saturday may be the most convenient day. On the other hand, if this consideration is not of overriding importance, there is something to be said for selecting some other day, so as to avoid the congested roads and crowded trains of the weekend.

With regard to the time. The Marriage Act (1934) permits marriages at any hour between 8 a.m. and 6 p.m. If a wedding is to be a very quiet one attended by only a very small number of people it is quite usual for it to take place early in the day, say, 10.30 a.m. When a fairly large number of guests have been invited, some of whom may have to travel some distance, a rather later hour is to be preferred. To hold a wedding at twelve would involve a large luncheon party afterwards. Consequently, 2.30 or 3.0 p.m. is the most popular time. This permits of a reception with wedding-cake and, perhaps, champagne after the ceremony; enables the newly-married couple to start off on their honeymoon before 5.0 p.m., and allows the guests to get home in good time. Such are some of the points that need to be borne in mind when fixing the time of a wedding ceremony.

Publishing the Banns of Marriage.—These are read or 'published' in Church on three Sundays preceding the ceremony. If the groom and bride live in separate parishes the banns must be published in both, the minister of the one church issuing a certificate stating that the banns have been so read, to be handed to the minister of the church in which the marriage is to take place. If, for some reason, the marriage is postponed so that three months have elapsed since the third reading, the banns cease to be valid and the parties will either have to obtain a licence or have the banns published again. These provisions may appear complicated to the layman, but they are familiar to any parish priest who can readily make clear what has to be done.

The Officiating Clergy.—Very often couples are married by the Vicar or Rector of the Church where the ceremony takes place. It is not for him to offer to officiate, so the couple concerned should make it plain when they discuss the arrangements with him that they would like him to marry them. It may be, however, that a couple wish the ceremony to be held in a particular church, but to be married by someone other than the vicar or rector of it, for example, by an old friend or relation of the groom or bride. The parish priest will readily understand this very natural wish, but it is, after all, 'his' church, so both as a matter of courtesy and to avoid confusion, he should be asked at an early stage to fall in with the proposed arrangement. It would be usual, in these circumstances, for the parish priest to take some part in the service, the visiting clergyman conducting the actual marriage ceremony. The two would, no doubt, discuss beforehand exactly what share each should have in the conduct of the service. Such an arrangement is not uncommon. Should the parents of the bride prepare for insertion in a local newspaper an account of the wedding, the relevant passage could be worded:—"The marriage ceremony was performed by Canon E. J. Sanders, uncle of the bride, assisted by the Vicar, the Rev. G. H. Carr." On occasions when the marriage ceremony is conducted by a family friend the engaged couple will probably give him a present of some kind. When the parish priest officiates he receives a fee for his services.

Music at the Marriage Service.—One point to be decided is whether the choir, or some members of it, are to take part in the service. This is a matter of taste, and to a small extent of expense, but it depends mainly on whether the wedding is to be a big affair and on the amount of music required. Nowadays the services of a choir are often dispensed with, but those of the organist are certainly essential. If neither the couple to be married nor the parents have any decided views on the hymns to be sung, they would be well advised to seek the advice of the parish priest and the organist.

The Form of Service.—If it is decided to have a printed form of service, as is often done except at quiet weddings, any psalms and hymns to be sung are printed together with the text of the marriage service, so that prayer-books and hymn-books are not needed by the congregation. It is scarcely necessary to add that the couple to be married should study the form of service carefully before the ceremony. Someone must be responsible for having the forms of service printed after discussion with the officiating priest and the organist, and must ensure that copies are available so that ushers at the church door can hand one to each member of the congregation.

Wedding Invitations.—When the date, time and place of the ceremony have been settled, the invitations to it can be prepared. For a very quiet wedding invitations may take the form of a personal letter. For others they are printed, not on cards, like invitations to dinners, but on the front of a double sheet of paper. Any good stationer will have a selection of such invitation forms and will undertake to print copies of the kind chosen. The wording usually runs as follows:—

Mr. and Mrs. Rupert Ellis
request the pleasure of the company
of

....

on the occasion of the marriage of their daughter
Mary
with (*or* to)
Mr. Roger Blake
on Wednesday, May 27th
at 2.30 p.m. at St. Botolph's Church, Camberley,
and
afterwards at the reception at The Crown Hotel,
Camberley.[1]

9, Hatchard Gardens,
Camberley.   R.S.V.P.

Sending Wedding Invitations.—It is usual to post the invitations about three or four weeks before the date of the wedding. The manner in which the names of the guests are set down is the same as for invitations to dinners or Sherry parties.

e.g. Sir Ronald and Lady Weeks,
     The Misses Soames.
     Mr. and Mrs. (John) Chaytor.

As the bride's parents rather than the bridegroom's are responsible for most of the wedding arrangements, the bride's parents will, in fact, send out the invitations, not only to their own friends and relations, but also to those of the bridegroom and his parents. It follows that groom and bride in consultation with their parents should draw up a list of people to be invited, and give the completed list to the bride's mother, who will see to it that the names are written in and the invitations sent.

[1] *Alternatively:*—"and afterwards, at 9, Hatchard Gardens."

Acknowledging a Wedding Invitation.—As the invitation is in the third person, the reply to it should also be in the third person.

e.g.

1.   Mr. and Mrs. John Chaytor accept with pleasure the kind invitation of Mr. and Mrs. Rupert Ellis to the marriage of their daughter Mary to Mr. Roger Blake at St. Botolph's Church, Camberley, on Wednesday, May 27th, and to the reception afterwards at The Crown Hotel.

2.   Mr. and Mrs. C. J. Arthur thank Mr. and Mrs. Rupert Ellis for their kind invitation to the wedding of their daughter Mary, but greatly regret they are unable to accept it as they are leaving for Italy next week.

Responsibility for Wedding Arrangements.—It is impossible to draw up a rigid scheme listing the various things to be done and showing who is to do them. One family may discuss and carry out arrangements as a kind of co-operative enterprise, while in another the bride's mother will do most of the work and her husband pay the resultant bills. Again, arrangements for one wedding may be elaborate, for another simple. In this book we have in mind a wedding with printed invitation cards and form of service, and a reception afterwards, because to describe the arrangements involved in such a function may be useful to a prospective bride and bridegroom and their relations. Some of the details therefore are not applicable to a very quiet wedding. But there is certainly no reason why a couple should not be married quietly if they wish. Indeed, before they decide on costly arrangements people would do well to consider whether a simpler one is preferable. A bride's parents may naturally wish to see

EGM—E

their daughter "married in style," but it is quite possible that the young couple would derive more lasting benefit from a quiet wedding and a substantial cheque as a parental wedding present. Ostentation is in bad taste and people ought not to spend more on a wedding than they can readily afford. On the other hand, a wedding is an important family occasion and, provided that foolish extravagances are avoided, there is no reason why it should not be celebrated accordingly.

That said, let us see, so far as is practicable, how the duties and responsibilities for a wedding in church and a reception afterwards might be distributed among the various people concerned.

Responsibilities of the Parents of the Bride.—These, as has already been mentioned, are considerable and, except perhaps in a financial sense, bear far more heavily on the bride's mother than on the father. Broadly speaking, the mother is likely to find herself responsible for practically everything connected with the preparations for the actual ceremony and for the reception afterwards. She will, of course, discuss plans with other people, listen to suggestions and depute certain people to do certain things, but in the last resort she is responsible for the smooth running of the whole affair. Some of the problems with which, directly or indirectly, she must grapple have already been mentioned. But there can be no harm in including them again in the general list. This—while allowing for differences between one wedding and another—would be likely to comprise the following:—

(*a*) Announcing the engagement in one or more newspapers.

(*b*) Settling the date, place and time of the wedding.

(*c*) Choosing the style of wedding invitation and ensuring that sufficient copies are ordered and received from the stationer's a month before the wedding.

(*d*) Compiling a list of the guests to be invited, completing the wedding invitations and sending them out, say, three weeks before the date of the wedding.

(*e*) Deciding on the form of the service and on the music to be played in consultation with the bridal couple, the officiating priest and the organist.

(*f*) Seeing that printed copies of the form of service are available for distribution by the ushers.

(*g*) Deciding how many front pews on either side of the central aisle of the church should be reserved for relatives or intimate friends, and providing the ushers with a list of the names of the people whom they should show into these places.

(*h*) Providing the bride's wedding dress and trousseau.

(*i*) Arranging for the decoration of the church. At fashionable weddings this is sometimes done by professional florists: otherwise by the bride's mother and her friends.

(*j*) Arranging for photographers to be present and deciding when and where photographs shall be taken.

(*k*) (if necessary) Making an additional list of guests to whom invitations have been sent to be given to the editor of a local newspaper who, not having a large staff of reporters, may be glad to have such information.

(*l*) Ordering cars:

    (i) To take the bride's mother (and others), the bridesmaids and the bride and her father to the church.

    (ii) To take the bridal couple, other relatives, the bridesmaids and perhaps one or two elderly people from the church to the reception.

    (iii) To take the bridegroom and the best man to the church. This is properly the former's responsibility, but it may be advisable for one person to hire all the cars.

    (iv) To take the newly-married pair from the reception to the station (unless, of course, they are going for a honeymoon by car).

    (v) To meet at and take back to the station a few selected guests known to be coming some distance by train. Such guests should be informed in advance that a car will meet certain trains. If cars have been ordered by telephone or word of mouth, this should be followed by a letter listing the requirements, and clearly stating the times at which cars are needed at the various points.

In addition to all this the bride's mother will have to consider the provision of meals before and after the wedding for relations and others. There is also the major matter of the reception. But consideration of this can better be postponed to a later page.

Expenses to be met by the Bridegroom.—In addition to giving a wedding present to his bride and buying the wedding ring, the bridegroom pays expenses connected with the actual marriage ceremony, for example, payments to the verger, the bell-ringers, the organist's fee (usually), and the fee of the clergyman who performs the marriage ceremony. If the officiating priest is a relative he may, instead, give him a present on behalf of his bride and himself.

The bridegroom does not pay for the decorations in the church, but he does pay for the bouquets carried by his bride and her bridesmaids, and for the best man's buttonhole as well as his own. He will also give a present to the bridesmaids and to the pages.

It is clear that the bulk of the expenditure falls on the parents of the bride. This is reasonable enough, for once she is married the bridegroom is responsible for making a home for his wife and for supporting her. Nowadays she may well contribute to the maintenance of the home, but the ultimate responsibility rests with her husband. Their joint resources may be increased by money settled on them at the time of the marriage by their respective parents, but that is a family matter and no concern of a book such as this.

The Bridesmaids.—The number of bridesmaids is a matter of choice. At a fashionable wedding they may number six or eight. For most weddings, however, the bride will be attended by two or four bridesmaids, with the possible addition of two small pages.

The bridesmaids are usually drawn from among the

sisters or other near relatives of the bride; sometimes also of the bridegroom. If friends of the bride are included, they ought not to replace her sisters. If the bride particularly wants one or two of her friends to act as bridesmaids, the solution is to increase the number of bridesmaids, so as to allow the inclusion both of sisters and of friends.

By custom, the bridesmaids are dressed alike (except for accessories). It is for the bride to choose the style, colour and material of her bridesmaids' dresses, though she will no doubt discuss the matter with them. The bridesmaids usually pay for their own dresses, though there is no reason why the bride's parents should not do so if they wish. As has been stated, the bridegroom pays for the bouquets carried by the bridesmaids, but these should be chosen with an eye to the colour of their dresses.

The Best Man.—It is for the bridegroom to choose the best man, who may be a brother or a close friend. If he comes down only on the wedding day or on the day before, there is not much for the best man to do, except to accompany the bridegroom to the church in good time, take charge of the wedding ring, hand it to him at the right moment, and escort the chief bridesmaid when the bridal party leaves the vestry on the way out of church. But if he is available in the days before the wedding, he can order cars and lend a useful hand with some of the other arrangements for which the bride's parents are responsible. He can also relieve the bridegroom of the task of paying the fees due to the parson, verger and others.

Rehearsals.—No piece of ceremonial can be carried out without a hitch unless it has been adequately rehearsed. When a wedding is on an elaborate scale it is essential therefore that those principally concerned should visit the church, though not, of course, in their wedding finery, and run through the order of proceedings, so that, for instance, the bridesmaids know where to stand when waiting for the bride to arrive, and that everyone knows when and where to stand or sit during the service, and how to reach the vestry for the signing of the register. Even for a simple wedding a preliminary visit to the church is desirable. Brides and bridegrooms may be nervous, and are much less liable to make mistakes if they have had the chance to run through the ceremony in advance and on the spot.

The Ushers.—Brothers and close friends of the bride and groom are obvious choices for this rôle. It is their business to show members of the congregation into their seats in the church, and to hand to each new arrival a copy of the Order of Service. It is essential that the ushers should be at their posts early, half an hour or more before the time fixed for the wedding. In particular, those on duty in the central aisle should, if possible, know many of the guests at least by sight. These ushers, and perhaps the others, should study in advance the lists drawn up by the bride's mother of those people who, being relatives or old friends of the bride or groom or of their parents, are to be given seats in the front pews.

People who are friends of the bride or her parents should be directed into the pews on the left (north) side of the aisle; friends of the groom or his family into pews on the right (south) side. If the church is well-filled the later arrivals will, of course, have to be shown into any seats still available no matter on which side. On being approached by an usher guests usually tell him whether they are friends of the bride or groom. If they do not, and he is in doubt, he should ask them himself. But his main duty is to ensure that the seats intended for the relatives of the couple are not occupied by other people.

Photographers.—A marriage in a church is a religious ceremony. It is irreverent and distasteful to have photographers taking flashlight photographs inside the church while the ceremony is in progress. We are considering here the marriage of two private individuals and not the

televising for the benefit of millions of outside viewers of some more august occasion. There is no reason why such photographs should not be taken in the vestry or of the couple emerging from the church or, for instance, at the reception, either by natural light in the garden, or by flashlight at the moment when the wedding cake is being cut. But it is offensive to see a photographer lurking in the choir stalls and flashing a bulb when the couple are kneeling before the officiating priest.

The wisest course is to give the photographers clear instructions to take photographs just outside the church porch and before or during the reception.

The Wedding Ceremony

Arriving at the Church.—The ushers should be at their posts, two by the porch, others in the various aisles, at least half an hour before the time fixed for the wedding. If it is raining, or looks showery, they should have an umbrella or two in the porch so that, in case of need, they can hold them over the bridesmaids and the bride, as they alight from cars.

The next to arrive should be the bridegroom and the best man. They can, if they wish, wait in the vestry, but when guests arrive they should both go and sit in the front pew on the right (south) side of the aisle, the best man sitting on the right of the groom. The organist will play the selections previously decided on as the church begins to fill up.

The bride's mother (and any others constituting her party) should be among the early arrivals and will sit, escorted thither by an usher, in the front pews on the left (north) side of the aisle. They may, in fact, choose the second pew, leaving the front one empty, as the corresponding pew on the right side will also be vacant when the groom and best man go to the chancel steps as the bride arrives at the church. The groom's parents should also arrive in good time and will sit level with the bride's mother but on the right (south) side of the aisle. Other relatives and friends for whom places have been reserved will be conducted by the ushers to seats on the right or left side, whichever is appropriate.

The bride, accompanied by her father (or, failing him, by another relative appointed to 'give her away') will be the last of the bridal party to arrive at the church. She should, if possible, reach the porch—where her bridesmaids are waiting—at the time appointed for the

EGM—E*

ceremony to begin or very soon after, because the period of waiting is a trying one for the bridegroom and to be late is always discourteous. The officiating clergy will be waiting just inside the church door and, as soon as the bride is ready, will walk slowly up the aisle. The organist, versed in these matters, will have arranged for somebody to give him his cue, if he himself has no direct view of the west end of the church. When the clergy begin to move forward he will either break into the wedding march from *Lohengrin* or weave a few bars of it into what he is playing, whereupon the congregation will stand.

The bride's father, giving his right arm to the bride, leads her up the church, the bridesmaids and pages following immediately behind. The bridegroom, meanwhile, will have taken his stand by the chancel steps, with the best man on his right, and he should turn to face the bride as her father leads her up the aisle towards him. The father then releases his daughter's arm and takes up a position a yard or so on her left and very slightly behind her. The bride, who will want to have her hands free during the service, hands her bouquet (and her gloves) to the chief bridesmaid. The best man now places himself to the right of, and slightly behind, the groom. The organist brings the 'voluntary' to a close, and the marriage service begins.

The Wedding Ceremony.—There is no need to describe the proceedings in detail. The clergyman who marries the couple will tell them in a low voice when to stand or kneel and when to get up and follow him to the altar rails. He will say, only a few words at a time, the sentences that each must repeat after him so that despite a natural nervousness neither of them should have any real difficulty.

When the clergyman asks "Who giveth this woman to this man?" the bride's father steps forward and says: "I do," after which he customarily joins his wife in her pew, or sits down in the vacant one in front of it. The best man, having handed the wedding ring to the groom when the clergyman indicates that he should do so, then steps back and may sit in the pew he had occupied with the groom before the entry of the bride. At the bidding of the clergyman the groom slips the ring on to the third finger of the bride's left hand (If this is more convenient she may, for this occasion, wear her engagement ring on her other hand). For sentimental reasons a bride sometimes chooses for her wedding ring an old one originally worn by, say, her grandmother. If her wedding ring is new it is likely to be of platinum rather than of gold, and much lighter than was formerly the fashion.

At the point in the service where the clergyman leads the couple to the altar rails—as is usual—the bridesmaids and pages continue to stand in the nave.

In the Vestry.—At the end of the service the bride takes the groom's left arm and goes with him into the vestry, the officiating priest leading the way. The best man conducts the chief bridesmaid there also. The remaining bridesmaids and the pages do not necessarily follow, particularly if the vestry is small, but the parents of the bride and groom leave their respective pews and go there. The rest of the congregation sit and the organist plays, while the newly-married couple sign the register— which is the legal evidence of their marriage—and receive the first congratulations from the others in the vestry.

Leaving the Church.—The organist, while playing, will have his eye on the vestry door. As soon as the bride and bridegroom are seen to leave the vestry, he begins to play the Wedding March (by Mendelssohn). Together, with the bride taking the left arm of the groom, the couple walk slowly down the aisle towards the porch and can smile at those whose glances they meet, as they advance. It is usual for the bride to wear her veil over her face when she enters the church but to wear it thrown back, as she comes out. The best man (who, in the vestry in addition to kissing the bride, may also have taken the opportunity to pay the parson on behalf of the bridegroom) comes next with the chief bridesmaid on his arm. The bride's mother follows with the bridegroom's father, and after them the groom's mother and the bride's father. They had entered the vestry as two couples, each man with his wife. They are now relatives by marriage and, to symbolize this, the father of each family walks down the church with the mother of the other. The remaining relations and others for whom seats had been reserved in the front pews come next, and only when they have all passed do the other members of the congregation leave their seats. The clergy (and the choir) do not take part in this procession down the aisle.

Outside the Church.—It is very likely that photographers will be waiting outside the church porch to take photographs of the bride and bridegroom and others of the bridal party. Members of the congregation should therefore stand aside while these pictures are being taken. If the reception is being held in a house or hotel some distance away, those who have been invited to it may now make their way there. If it is a short walking distance, they should wait until the bride and groom, their parents, and bridesmaids have already started. At all events the guests must allow the bride's parents time to get to the scene of the reception so that they may be ready to welcome their guests.

The best man and the ushers can be of assistance in helping those who are going to the reception into the cars already ordered for that purpose. At a country wedding, of course, everyone may walk the short distance from the village church to the house where the reception is being held. But in towns some cars will certainly be necessary.

The bride and groom travel in the first, the bridesmaids (and pages), the parents of the newly married couple in others. If one or two guests, not strictly included in the bridal party, have been promised a lift because they are old or infirm, the bride's mother (or some other responsible person) should make sure that an additional car has been ordered, and ask one of the ushers beforehand to see them in to it. Strictly, the best man should travel with the chief bridesmaid, but it may be more convenient if she goes with the other bridesmaids, leaving him free to superintend the departure of the cars, pay the verger and bell-ringers for their services, if he has not done so already, and to do anything else that may be necessary, before he himself goes to the reception.

The Reception

Making Arrangements.—The wedding reception may be held in a hotel or at the home of the bride's parents. Wherever it may be, it is wise, unless the wedding is a very quiet one attended by only a small number of near relatives, to entrust the arrangements to a reliable firm of caterers.

Employing a Caterer.—The advantages of doing so are great. Few people have adequate domestic help nowadays, and the hostess during the time before the wedding will have more than enough to do without having to provide food and drink, glasses and cutlery, etc. for at least fifty people and probably more. No doubt, expense has to be considered, but a wedding is, after all, a very special and infrequent occasion, and the extra cost of paying a caterer to do everything instead of trying to cope with it oneself, is offset by the enormous saving of worry and trouble at what must inevitably be a very busy time for the bride's parents. "Be reasonable, Madam! If you will have to hire glasses and plates because you are unlikely to have enough of your own and cannot possibly find time to make the eatables you propose to offer to your guests, surely it is better to put the whole business into the hands of people who are far more used to this kind of thing than you are."

If the reception is to be held at a hotel, the first step to take is to ascertain whether the manager is prepared, not only to set aside one or more rooms for the reception, but also to provide all the refreshments and the staff to serve them. A big hotel may be able to undertake everything connected with the reception. At a smaller one the manager may prefer to do no more than make accommodation available, leaving the refreshments and necessary staff to be provided by the caterer. In that case, it is a matter of settling with the caterer what food and drink he should provide, and leaving him to discuss the arrangements with the manager of the hotel.

A Wedding Reception at a Private House.—After a very small wedding, attended almost exclusively by near relatives, instead of a reception there would be an informal family gathering, at which the wedding cake would be cut, healths drunk, and refreshments provided, their kind depending on the time of day.

For purposes of this book, however, we are assuming that a number of friends as well as relations attended the ceremony and that, since the wedding took place at 2.30 p.m., there is to be an afternoon reception. Further, as there will be a good many guests, the aid of a caterer has been enlisted, and the reception is to take place at the house of the bride's parents.

Such a reception is held in whichever room is the largest and most convenient for the purpose, or, better still, in two inter-communicable rooms. Alternatively, if the house has a garden, the reception can perhaps take place in a marquee set up by the caterer with, as a precaution against rain, an awning leading from the garden gate to the marquee and, possibly, from it to the door of the house.

Receiving the Guests.—Those of the men who are in morning dress with top hats will be thankful to put them down. The bride's mother therefore should appoint someone, preferably one of her own domestic staff, whether permanent or an obliging 'daily', to take charge of the men's hats and, if there are many, to issue a numbered ticket in exchange for each, just as in a public cloak-room. The ladies, too, may be glad of somewhere to leave their things.

The bride's mother and father wait inside the door of the reception room or near the entrance to the marquee to welcome their guests as they arrive. A servant, one of the caterer's staff, may be posted to announce the names, but this is not necessary unless the reception is a large one.

Next to the bride's parents stand those of the bride-groom, and beside them the newly married couple. The guests shake hands with these six people, and express their good wishes and congratulations as they do so. A few words will suffice, after which the guests should pass on and not linger near the entrance, as this would bar the way of others following on and wishing also to pay their respects.

Refreshments.—As soon as the guests begin to arrive the caterer's staff should begin to serve refreshments. The hostess will have discussed with the caterer what is to be provided. He will quote a price per head which will vary according to the kind of food and drink served. He will also provide all the glasses, plates, cutlery and tables required. It is true that champagne is considered the most suitable beverage in which to drink the health of the bride and bridegroom. There is no denying, however, that for a large company it is expensive. If the bride's parents are of modest means they must not feel under any obligation to provide champagne. Cider cup, claret cup or champagne cup are perfectly acceptable alternatives, and soft drinks should also be available for teetotallers. The eatables usually take the form of sandwiches, small sausage rolls and other things of the kind served at cocktail parties. Sometimes tea or coffee is served when the guests first arrive, champagne being served later shortly before the wedding cake is cut.

The Wedding Cake.—This is prominently displayed on a table in the centre of the room or marquee. When the reception is in full swing, but not before, the bride, assisted by the bridegroom, cuts the first slice. Sometimes the best man or the bride's father will announce:— "The bride will now cut the cake", and the guests will clap as she does so, but this is not necessary, because the cake is so prominent an object that those present cannot fail to observe the couple as they approach it. Often flashlight photographs are taken at the moment of cutting the cake.

The bride is not expected to do more than cut the first slice, one of the caterer's staff then taking over the task. Small slices are carried round on dishes, so that each guest may have one. Champagne (or whatever other drink has been selected) will then be served, if this has not already been done, because now is the time for proposing healths.

To friends who were invited to the reception but who were unable to come small slices of wedding cake should subsequently be sent. A stationer can provide boxes of a suitable size to hold a small slice together with a small piece of paper, the size of a visiting card, on which is printed the name of the newly married couple. The boxes can be sent by post any time after the wedding, and it is helpful to keep a list of people (particularly if they have given wedding presents) to whom a slice of wedding cake is to be sent.

Speeches.—At a wedding reception the speeches should be short. Someone—it may be the bride's father or an old friend of the family—must propose the health of the bride and bridegroom, and will earn full marks if he does so with a touch of humour, genuine sincerity, good will and brevity. The bridegroom responds to this toast on behalf of his wife and himself. Ideally, he should in his speech thank the bride's parents, whose shoulders have borne the main burden of the wedding preparations, refer to the bridesmaids (who look so charming), to the best man (who has been so efficient), and thank the guests for their presents and good wishes. But he can safely count on the good will of the company, and no one will think any the worse of him if he does no more than murmur a few words of thanks. If he does mention the bridesmaids, it would then be for the best man to reply on their behalf and on his own, but no other speeches are either necessary or desirable.

Departure of the Bride and Bridegroom.—After these speeches, which will probably be made about an hour after the beginning of the reception, the bride and bridegroom leave the reception room and go upstairs to change into their 'going-away clothes'. At the risk of being obvious it should here be pointed out that, on the previous day or at some suitable time in advance, the bridegroom must send to the house of the bride's parents or to wherever the reception is being held, not only the suit into which he is to change on leaving the reception but also, ready packed, the luggage he intends to take with him on the honeymoon.

Viewing the Wedding Presents.—Guests at a reception should not, without good reason, leave before the bride and bridegroom. While they are waiting for the couple to set off on their honeymoon, the guests may be invited to fill in the time by looking at the wedding presents set out in another room. As was explained in an earlier chapter a card should be affixed to each present giving the name of the donor and, on a separate list, the names of those who have given cheques.

This display of wedding presents is set out only in a private house, for if the reception is held in a hotel it would scarcely be practicable to transport all the presents there. If it is felt that people ought, nevertheless, to have an opportunity of seeing the presents, the solution is for the bride's mother to give tea parties on one or two afternoons before the wedding, so that those who come may then see the presents.

Departure for the Honeymoon.—Having changed into their going-away clothes and having had their luggage carried down to a waiting car or the taxi previously ordered, the newly married couple take leave of their near relations, but are not required to say goodbye individually to the guests at the reception. These latter may gather near the car to speed them on their way. The old custom of throwing rice and tying shoes to the back of the car is no longer fashionable, though it is still sometimes done. The same holds good of throwing confetti at the bridal couple as they come out of church. There is no harm in it, but it is seldom done at fashionable weddings, partly because it is untidy and gives the verger extra work.

The reception ends with the departure of the bride and bridegroom and all guests should then say goodbye to their hostess and take their leave.

Looking after the Staff.—The bride's mother should see to it that any of her own domestic staff who have helped at the reception should themselves have a slice of wedding cake and something to drink when the guests have left.

Wedding Anniversaries.—The only wedding anniversaries calling for more than purely family celebrations are those marking the 25th anniversary of the wedding day (Silver Wedding), the 50th anniversary (Golden Wedding) and the 60th anniversary (Diamond Wedding). As the names imply presents given in honour of these occasions, may appropriately take the form of a piece of plate or jewellery. In practice, only the nearest relatives give presents of so costly a nature, friends being required to do no more than write letters of congratulation or send gifts of flowers in recognition of such occasions.

The married couple may themselves like to insert in

the papers a notice of a major anniversary, the following being the usual form of words:—

Silver Wedding

Cooper: Harvey. On 14th November, 19— at Holy Trinity Church, Ealing, Cyril George Cooper to Joan Harvey (*or* Joan, younger daughter of the late Captain and Mrs. Harvey). Present address: The Moorings, Wroxham, Norfolk.

CHAPTER IX

BIRTHS AND CHRISTENINGS

Registering a Birth

The birth of a child must be registered at the office of the local Registrar. The law requires that this be done within 42 days (in Scotland 21 days) of the infant's birth. No charge is made provided that the birth is registered within the period prescribed. Usually the birth is registered within a few days of its happening, the father being the person to do it.

Announcing a Birth

As with engagements, a birth is made known to near relations by letter or telephone. There is no necessity to announce a birth in a newspaper, but most parents like to do so in, say, *The Daily Telegraph* and/or *The Times* or perhaps only in a local paper. No matter in what paper it appears, a cheque should be sent to the Editor with the notice for insertion. Every newspaper quotes its charges for such items. By comparing the length of the proposed notice with that of another already published in the paper concerned it is easy to arrive at a fairly accurate estimate of the cost.

Form of Announcement

The wording varies only within narrow limits as the following examples will show:—

1. Jones. On October 18th, 19— to Mr. and Mrs. Robert Jones of Orchard House, Petersfield—a son.
2. Bates. On June 7th, 19— at The Cottage Hospital,

Henfield to Mary (*née* Croft) and Thomas H. Bates
—a daughter (Winifred Joan).

3. Curtis. On July 12th, 19— To Christine, wife of
   Captain R. S. Curtis, of Glynde, near Lewes,
   Sussex, the gift of a daughter.

4. Robinson. On February 5th, 19— To Daphne (*née*
   McLeod) and Charles Robinson—a brother for
   John, Sybil and Richard.

One often comes across a notice in the style of the
last example, but it has two unsatisfactory features. We
may not need to know whether the baby was born in the
home of its parents or in a hospital or nursing home,
but if no address at all is given, misunderstanding can
arise since other parents may have the same surname
and even Christian names as those to whom the notice
refers. It is therefore better to state where the parents
live. Secondly, the last notice is rather unkind to the
new baby because he seems to be welcome less on his
own account than as a companion to his parents' other
children. If they wish to proclaim to all and sundry that
the new arrival is not their first-born they can make this
clear while giving the new baby his fair share of the
notice by altering the last part to "—a son (George
William), a brother for John, Sybil and Richard."
After all, we don't get our name in the papers often, and
it's a pity to miss so good an opportunity.

A Word of Warning

In recent years some parents have adopted a practice,
fairly widespread on the Continent, of informing their
friends of the birth of a son or daughter by means of a
printed card. There is no reason why this should not be
done, but a plain card stating simply that "so and so" have

pleasure in announcing the birth of a son (or daughter), named "such and such" on a given date is preferable to one which achieves a regrettable coyness by purporting to be sent by a new-born infant. These effusions usually show a stork carrying a baby and some painfully arch wording: e.g. "Allow me to introduce myself. I am James Henry Smith and when I arrived on 27th November: I weighed 7 lb. Wasn't that clever of me? Mummy and Daddy think I'm rather sweet and I hope you will too."

Much can be forgiven to proud parents, but not whimsies of this sort.

Replying to an Announcement

Friends of the parents will naturally wish to congratulate them on the birth of the baby. Intimate friends may, if they wish, send flowers accompanied by a brief note. There is no set form for letters of this kind. They need not be long and might be expressed in the following terms:—

Dear Mrs. Cooper,

I was delighted to read in *The Times* two days ago that you have a little son, and hasten to send you my hearty congratulations. I shall very much look forward to making his acquaintance one of these days. Meanwhile, my best wishes to him— and to you all,

Yours sincerely,

Godparents

As the word implies godparents have some responsibility for the spiritual welfare of the child on whose behalf they act, and are supposed to see that the infant is instructed in the faith of the Church to which he is admitted at his baptism. There is no denying that nowadays, when many people go to church less regularly than did their forefathers, this aspect of a godparent's duties is often neglected. Many godparents content themselves with keeping an occasional eye on their godchild until he is grown up and feel that they have done all that is expected of them if they remember him on his birthday, and give him a final present when he reaches the age of twenty-one.

The seriousness with which godparents take their duties therefore varies a good deal, but it is helpful to any child to have someone outside the immediate family circle to show a personal interest in him, and it is a compliment to be asked to be a godparent.

Godparents are sometimes relations of the child's father and mother. Very often they are old and trusted friends. If the child concerned is a boy it is customary for him to have two godfathers and one godmother: if a girl, two godmothers and one godfather. The godparents generally give a christening present to the child, sometimes in the form of a silver Christening mug, often by sending a sum of money with the request that it should be used to open an account for the child in the Post Office Savings Bank. Sometimes a godfather will include a godchild among the beneficiaries of his will, but there is no obligation, legal or moral, for him to do so. His responsibilities, such as they are, cease altogether when the godchild comes of age.

An Invitation to act as Godfather

My dear John,

    You are one of my oldest friends and I should

in fact have asked you to be best man at my wedding, had you not been abroad at the time. I am writing now to ask whether you would stand as godfather to our son, who will be christened some time next month. Mary agrees with me that you are just the person we should like to have, so I hope very much that you will consent. It would please us both immensely.

Yours ever,
Frank.

The Reply

My dear Frank,

From a worldly point of view your son would do better to have a more prosperous godfather than myself! But I take it very kindly that you should think me suitable for that office, and I am proud to accept. I shall be moving about on business during part of next month, but if you will let me know the date of the christening fairly soon, I will try to arrange to be free on that day. I believe it is not absolutely essential for all the godparents to be present on that occasion, but I hope I can manage it. The sooner I make the acquaintance of my godchild the better. My love to Mary.

Yours ever,
John.

P.S. I don't have to carry the infant, do I?

Arranging the Christening

As the majority of people in this country are members of the Church of England, we will assume here that the baby is to be christened in a parish church. In fact, to whatever religious denomination the parents belong, the first step they must take is to arrange with the priest or minister the date and time of the ceremony.

In former times when the rate of infant mortality was very high it was usual for a baby to be baptised very soon after his birth, lest he should die before being received into the Church. Nowadays, provided that the baby is healthy, the Christening may take place some weeks or even a month or two after his birth, but it is advisable to fix the date well in advance.

Invitations to a Christening

Even though the wedding of the parents may have been an elaborate one, the christening of their child is likely to be a much simpler affair, attended only by relatives and a small number of intimate friends. For such an essentially family occasion printed invitations will probably not be needed. If they should be, the invitation would be expressed in the third person in the usual way, e.g.:—

Mr. and Mrs. Charles Harper

request the pleasure of the company

of

....

on Sunday, 19th June, at 2.30 p.m.

at St. Sebastian's Church, Dorking,

on the occasion of the christening of their son,

and afterwards (to tea)

at 28, Long Road, Dorking.

28, Long Road,   R.S.V.P.

Dorking.

Usually, however, only a few people will be invited,

and this can be done without too much trouble by means of personal letters, e.g.:—

My dear X,

On Sunday, 19th June, our baby is to be christened at St. Sebastian's Church here at 2.30 p.m. Both Frank and I hope very much that you will be able to be there, and to come back to tea with us afterwards. We shall only be quite a small party, and shall be delighted to include you in it.

Yours affectionately,

Mary.

Choosing the Names

Before the child is born the parents-to-be have probably decided what names they mean to give him or her. They have every right to make their own decision, but having chosen the first name, the one by which the child will usually be called, they might pause to consider the pleasure it might give to near relatives if they chose the remaining names from among those already borne by other members of the family. A single Christian name is meagre; four or more are excessive unless it is a family custom. Two or three names are the usual number. While it is certainly right for parents to consult their own wishes and those of their relations in this matter, they might also take into account the feelings of the child. If, say, Aubrey and Marmaduke are names that have occurred for generations in the family, by all means perpetuate them. The son may well be glad that he bears them—when he grows up. But unless there is a good reason for choosing them, parents should think twice before saddling a child with names which, during his early school days at least, are liable to cause him

agonies of resentful embarrassment. Ornaments of the
stage and screen often assume for professional purposes
exotic and unusual names. But these have their day, and
it is trying for a child to go through life burdened with
names such as Gloria, Rudolph, Marlon or Sabrina,
which, however suitable for film stars, are likely to be
incongruous or wildly inappropriate in other walks of
life. There is a good deal to be said for the more ordinary
names.

At the Church

The godparents should, if possible, be present at the
christening, but the ceremony can be carried out in their
absence, if need be, the mother herself acting as godmother. Assuming that they are able to attend, the
godparents together with the parents and other near
relatives will group themselves round the font, while
friends will probably sit in the pews near by. The godmother (or one of the two, if the baby is a girl) will
stand on the left of the officiating clergyman, holding
the child in her arms. The godfathers have little to do
beyond saying: "I renounce them all," on being asked
by the priest in the course of the service whether, on
behalf of the child, they renounce the devil and all his
works. At the appropriate moment the parson takes the
child from the godparent and asks what names are to be
given to the baby. It is usual for the father to supply the
information and he should do so clearly. After the child
has been christened the priest hands him back to the
godmother. The service is not long. When it is over the
father goes to the vestry with the clergyman so that the
particulars may be recorded in the register. It is usual
for him then to make an offering to the church funds,

and to give something to the verger. If he is uncertain how much he should give, he should ask the advice of the priest.

After the Christening

If the clergyman who christened the child is a friend of the family, he will no doubt be asked to tea after the ceremony. It is customary to have a christening cake, but no other special arrangements are made. A 'stand-up' tea with the tea things on a side table in one corner and a few chairs for the older people can be arranged if the room would otherwise be uncomfortably crowded. Any christening presents given to the baby can be set out if desired. In most cases a christening is a family affair which does not call for elaborate preparations.

CHAPTER X

FUNERALS

Funerals

Before broaching this necessary but inevitably depressing subject, it will be advisable to deal very briefly with the legal aspect.

Registering a Death

The law requires that the local Registrar of Births and Deaths be notified of a death not more than five days after its occurrence. This must be done either by a relative who was present when the person died, by some other relative, or by the occupier or by an inmate of the house in which the death took place. Whoever notifies the Registrar must sign the Register in his presence. The Registrar must also receive a certificate of the cause of death signed by the doctor who attended the deceased during his last illness. The doctor may hand the certificate to the relative who is going to the Registrar's office to notify him of the death, or he may send it to the Registrar himself. The Registrar then issues a certificate which is, in effect, an authorisation for burial to take place. The undertaker usually takes charge of this certificate and gives it to the clergyman who is to conduct the funeral ceremony, or to the superintendent of the cemetery where the body is to be interred. In cases of death by accident or from unknown causes the circumstances would be reported by the doctor, the hospital authorities or the police to the local Coroner, and permission to bury would not be granted until an inquest had been held.

Making a Will

The prospect of dying is not an agreeable one to contemplate. It is perhaps for this reason that some people shrink from making a will or from discussing even with their nearest relatives the future of the family. Such reluctance is understandable, but unwittingly selfish. Death in putting an end to a life brings sorrow to those to whom the dead person was dear. At best it will be a sad time for them, and a thoughtful person would not wish to add to their burden by leaving them unnecessarily in doubt as to their financial position, or in uncertainty about how best to carry out his wishes. Anyone ought therefore to leave his affairs in as good order as possible. Not only should he make a will, he should also ensure that his executors know where it is kept, who his lawyers are, the address of his bank and where his stocks and share certificates are to be found. He should also leave a list of any personal belongings, not mentioned in his will, which he would like to be given to individuals as tokens of remembrance and friendship. Such 'wishes' are not binding in law, but they are an indication of thoughtfulness, and often a great help to a bereaved widow who would like old friends to have something in memory of her husband, but who would otherwise be uncertain what to do. There is nothing morbid about making such preparations. On the contrary to do so is both sensible and considerate.

The Place of Burial

If someone has a particular wish to be buried in a

certain churchyard or cemetery, he should either inform his nearest relations or his executors of his wish, or else mention it in his will or at least leave a memorandum among his private papers. If he has no strong feelings about it, he need do none of these things, but neglect even to discuss such matters may add to the natural sorrow of a widow a further worry because she does not know what he would have wished.

Cremation

Most people are buried in a parish churchyard or in a municipal cemetery. In recent years, however, an increasingly large number have expressed a wish for cremation. It is important that they should make this desire known in advance either by word of mouth or in writing. Readers of detective novels will know that traces of certain poisons, such as arsenic, can be identified in human remains exhumed months after burial. Cremation destroys such traces. It is understandable therefore that the law insists on certain safeguards. One is that in addition to the usual death certificate signed by the patient's doctor, a confirmatory one must be given by a second doctor, who need not have attended the patient in his lifetime, but who should see the body after death. If the relatives know in advance that the deceased had a preference for cremation, they are in a position to inform the family doctor, who can then readily arrange for a professional colleague to sign the additional certificate required.

There is no need to prolong these observations. These various formalities are unpleasant, the more so as they must be dealt with at a time of sorrow. Relatives should therefore bear in mind that undertakers, by the very nature of their work, know what has to be done and consultation with them can make things easier for the bereaved.

The Type of Funeral Ceremony

Death is a solemn event, inspiring not only grief but awe. It is natural therefore that long before Christian times and among all races, throughout the world, the disposal of a body was accompanied by special rites and by actions of symbolic significance. When Shakespeare wrote that "nothing in his life became him like the leaving it" he was alluding to the redeeming courage with which the traitorous thane of Cawdor met his end. The words might equally well apply to the elaborate ceremonial with which funerals have often been carried out.

Among the very poor to be "buried by the parish" —that is, to have a pauper's funeral—was long regarded as the most humiliating experience and therefore to be prevented at any price. Thus, when death came to the head of the family, the survivors, often rendering themselves almost destitute by meeting the expenses, would derive a melancholy pride and satisfaction from the fact that the number of carriages following the coffin exceeded that to be seen in the funeral cortège of a neighbour.

Until recently it was thought fitting in the upper and middle classes for a funeral to be elaborate. The heads of the horses drawing the hearse were decked with plumes of black ostrich feathers. Hired mourners or 'mutes' accompanied the hearse, which was followed by a long line of sombre carriages. The near relatives of the deceased went into deep mourning for six months or a

EGM—F

year, and then into 'half-mourning'. The notepaper they used had a black border diminishing in width as the months went by.

Such customs have now very largely disappeared. The reason may be that scarcely a family in the country did not lose at least one of its members in the first World War, and the men who fell were buried in the countries where they died. Their relatives had, nevertheless, to carry on, and in the inter-war years there was no reversion to the elaborate procedure of earlier days. It was not so much that life had become cheap as that, for many people, there was something distasteful about the trappings and paraphernalia of elaborate funerals. Whatever the reason, the trend now is towards a ceremony which remains reverent and dignified and yet is simple.

Announcement of a Death

In addition to notifying the Registrar, as the law requires, the relatives will wish to inform their friends of what has taken place. No doubt they will let near relations know by letter or telephone, since it would come as a shock to those most closely concerned if the first intimation they had of the death of a near relative were to be an impersonal notice in a newspaper.

Such an announcement will nevertheless be needed for the benefit of others who are outside the immediate family circle. Before preparing a notice for insertion in the *Daily Telegraph*, *The Times* or in a local newspaper, various points must first be considered, since the wording of the notice will depend to some extent on the decision reached about them. Among these matters for consideration are:—

(*a*) Was it the known wish of the dead person, or is it the wish, say, of his widow that only members of the family should attend the funeral?

(*b*) Did the dead man express a wish for a very quiet funeral, without signs of mourning or flowers?

(*c*) Did the dead man wish to be buried in the place where he was born and not in the place where he spent the latter part of his life? If so, should there be a Memorial Service in the church of the parish where he lived?

(*d*) Should there be only one notice? Or should the first announcing his death be followed by a second giving details of the time and place of the funeral?

(*e*) Where should flowers and wreaths be sent?

(*f*) If friends are likely to come from a distance to attend the funeral, what time should the ceremony be held to enable them to do so?

(*g*) If the body is to be cremated, should the whole service be held at the crematorium, or should the first part of the funeral service take place in church?

(*h*) Should the age of the deceased be given, and should any mention be made in the notice of his parents or of his widow and children?

(*i*) Should any mention be made of the length of his last illness?

It is clear from the above that, although notices of death follow broadly the same lines, their form does admit of some variation. When the wording has been settled, the notice should be sent to the editor of the paper. A cheque to cover the cost of its insertion should accompany the notice, failing which its insertion may be delayed. Newspapers mention their charges for notices of this kind, so that by comparing the length of the proposed notice with that of one already published in the particular paper, it is easy to arrive at a sufficiently accurate estimate of the cost.

Specimen Announcements of a Death

The following examples take into account the various points that have been mentioned on page 163, and show how the wording of an announcement can be varied so as to bring in some of the points while excluding others according to circumstances.

1. Smith. On 26th November, 19—, John Marston, of Longwood, Ventnor, I.W., youngest son of the late Mr. and Mrs. J. H. Smith of Wimbledon, and formerly Chairman of the firm of Smith and Marston Ltd., of Paddington.

2. Smith. On 26th November, 19—, Lily Joan, of Copse Farm, near Taunton, widow of Lt.-Colonel F. H. Smith, Royal Artillery, in her 82nd year. Funeral service at St. Columba's Church, Taunton, on Tuesday, 30th November, at 2.30 p.m. Cut flowers to Farmer, Funeral Director, Taunton.

3. Smith. On 26th November, 19—, suddenly, at Highfields, Sedlescombe, George Martin, beloved husband of Dorothy May Smith, and father of Roderick Smith and Daphne White, in his 65th year. Cremation will take place privately. Memorial Service at Sedlescombe Parish Church, on Tuesday, 2nd December, at 2.30 p.m.

4. Smith. On 26th November, 19—, after a long illness courageously borne, Humphrey James Smith of Temple House, Hove, aged 75. Funeral Service at St. Sepulchre's Church, Brighton, on 30th

November, at 2.0 p.m. No flowers and no mourning at his request.

5.   Smith. On 26th November, 19—, as the result of an accident Peter, dearly loved only child of Dr. and Mrs. R. H. Smith of 12, Avenue Road, Ealing. Service at St. Dunstan's Church, Ealing, on 1st December, at 2.0. p.m. No flowers, please, but donations may be sent instead to the N.S.P.C.C.

6.   Smith. On 26th November, 19—, peacefully, at his home at Dorking, Nicholas John Smith, very dear husband of Elizabeth. Cremation private. Memorial Service to be announced later. Please, no letters.

Letters of Condolence

Every consideration should be shown for the members of a family who have just suffered a bereavement. In particular, if they definitely ask in a newspaper announcement that their friends should refrain from writing to them, this wish should be respected. The reason for the request is not that they are indifferent to the bereavement, but rather that to receive expressions of sympathy would undermine the composure which they are striving to maintain, and which they must preserve if they are to come through the ordeal of dealing with all the arrangements for the funeral, while they are overwhelmed with grief at the loss they have sustained. If there has been no mention of letters in the newspaper announcement, friends will naturally wish to write. Very intimate friends will know how to find suitable words. For those who do not know the family so well the task may be more difficult. One cannot lay down hard and fast rules, but one can safely recommend that such letters should be sincere, restrained and short, rather than gushing and lengthy.

Specimen Letters of Condolence

1. Dear Mrs. Hall,

I was extremely sorry to read in *The Times* of the sad death of your husband. I was at school with him, and I remember very clearly how popular he was. In later years I met him only occasionally, but he was always as friendly and cheerful as in the old days. Please accept my deepest sympathy in your great loss.

Yours sincerely,
John Forster.

2. My dear James,

The death of your Mother cannot have come altogether as a surprise, for I know she had been seriously ill for a long time. I am glad for her sake that she is now free of the pain and discomfort which she bore so uncomplainingly, but you and the other members of the family will, I know, miss her sadly—as, indeed, will all of us who had the privilege of her friendship.

With my very sincere sympathy,
Yours ever,
Eleanor.

Acknowledging Letters of Condolence

No one expects an immediate reply to a letter written to convey sympathy to a person who has just lost a near and dear relation, for the writer will know that the recipient will neither have the time to acknowledge such a letter—probably one of many—at once, nor be in a suitable frame of mind to deal with such correspondence.

Meanwhile, as a practical step, the members of the household, to one or other of whom letters of condolence have been sent, should make a list of those who have written, and keep all the letters together, so that they can be answered or acknowledged after the funeral. It was suggested above that letters of condolence from friends should usually be short. So, also, should the answers, which might be worded in some such way as follows:—

1. Dear Mr. Forster,

It was very good of you to write. People have been wonderfully kind, and their sympathy has been a great comfort to me during these sad days. My husband often spoke of you and others of his schoolfriends, and always regretted that he had not been able to keep more closely in touch with them. Thank you once again for your kind letter.

Yours sincerely,

Mary Hall.

2. My dear Eleanor,

I am most grateful for your kind and understanding letter. We had known for a long time that Mother was not going to get better, but she was always so bright and interested in everything that, although I am thankful that her sufferings are at an end, her passing has left a gap in our lives which will be impossible to fill. You know as well as I do what she meant to us all, and I have no need to tell you how fond she was of you.

Yours ever,

James.

Sometimes, perhaps because they are elderly or infirm, the bereaved relatives find that the task of replying to a large number of letters of condolence is beyond their powers. In that case, they need answer personally only those from members of their intimate circle, and send to other friends or acquaintances a printed form of acknowledgement, to some of which they may add a word or two in their own handwriting if they wish. The wording of such a form of acknowledgement might be as follows:—

Mrs. and Miss Huxtable
deeply appreciate your sympathy,
and thank you for your very kind letter.

67, Marsden Road,
Bedford.   December, 19—.

An alternative method is to insert an announcement in the personal column of a newspaper in some such form as this:—

Mrs. and Miss Huxtable of 67, Marsden Road, Bedford, are deeply grateful for the many expressions of sympathy they have received from friends following their recent sad loss. They hope later to answer all these kind letters and know that, should they be unable to do so for some time, their friends will understand.

Note. The second sentence of this announcement might be omitted.

Preparations for the Funeral

It is usual for a person's funeral to take place some four or five days after his death. It follows that, however painful the necessity, the relatives have a good deal to do almost immediately after one of the family has died.

If the father of a family dies, leaving a widow and several small children, the main burden will necessarily fall on the widow. It may be that, to occupy her mind and to avoid thinking too much of her loss until she is better prepared to face it, the widow will find relief in being kept busy. Even so, if she has a brother or other male relative, she would be well advised to send for him at once. In a family where the children are grown up, they can be of great help in various ways.

The first step, as has already been indicated, is to decide the time, place and manner of the funeral, and to make sure that the church where the service is to be held is available at the time chosen. Announcements containing the necessary particulars must then be drawn up and sent to the newspapers, and letters or telegrams despatched to near relations.

This done, someone, preferably a grown up son or brother, should register the death and get in touch with the undertaker. With him he must settle such gloomy but necessary details as the type of coffin, when the body is to be removed to the mortuary chapel from the house or hospital where death took place, and the probable number of cars likely to be needed to convey relations from the house of the dead person and back again after the ceremony.

Most people nowadays live in towns. It is likely therefore that the first part of a funeral service will take place in church, the second by the graveside in a municipal cemetery. Sometimes a family, particularly one resident in a town for a number of years, will have purchased a plot of ground in a local cemetery large enough for several members of it to be buried there. In matters of this kind an undertaker can be of assistance. He can find out from the superintendent of the cemetery whether there is a family grave, whether there is space in it for the burial of another person, or whether interment should take place in another part of the cemetery. Enquiries of this kind are distressing, but necessary. Hence the desirability of a male relative, rather than the widow, making them, hence, too, the reason for consulting the undertaker, whose personal feelings are not involved, but who, by reason of his profession, knows exactly what has to be done.

Meanwhile other duties devolve on the female side of the bereaved family. Among them will be keeping a list of those who write letters of condolence, possibly replying at once to those written by a few very intimate friends, putting aside others to be answered later; perhaps arranging for the accommodation of relatives coming from a distance, and for conveying people by car from the house to the funeral and back. There will also be the necessary business of providing a meal for some members of the family before the funeral, while some kind of a buffet meal will be needed when the party return to the house before they disperse to their several homes. If the parson, doctor and lawyer are friends of the family, there is no reason why they should not be invited, but this is purely a matter of choice.

The Form of Service

Sometimes the undertaker will provide a few small bound copies of the funeral service bearing the name and dates of birth and death of the deceased, which he will hand to relatives before they go to the church. The provision of these is a matter of arrangement between the undertaker and the member of the family who has dealings with him. When a large number of friends are expected to attend the funeral, and more particularly when the funeral itself is private and a memorial service is held a few days later, it is usual to have a printed order of service, copies of which are placed in the pews beforehand for the use of the congregation. The service itself follows the lines laid down in the Prayer Book, but the psalms and hymns to be sung and, sometimes, the Lesson to be read can be chosen in accordance with the wishes of the family. To allow sufficient time for copies to be printed, it is essential that, as soon as the date of the funeral has been fixed, the form of the Service should be discussed with the parish priest. Similarly, if a member of the family or a close friend in Holy Orders is to officiate or take part in the Service, the Vicar or Rector of the Church must be consulted, so that the allocation of duties between the two is made clear. He will also wish to know whether, as would be usual, the choir is to take part. A member of the family may make himself responsible for the printing of the Form of Service. Alternatively, the undertaker may be instructed to see to it.

Flowers

Where the notice in the newspapers includes the words "No Flowers" this request should be respected by friends. In its absence they are free to send flowers as a token of sympathy and respect. Sometimes the newspaper announcement gives the name and address of the undertaker, in which case the inference is that flowers should be sent to that address. If no such information is given, it is reasonable to assume that these tributes should be sent to the home of the bereaved family. People sending flowers from their own garden should attach a card to their gift. Those having flowers delivered by a florist should leave a card with the florist when they order the flowers. The undertaker should be asked to make a list of those who send flowers to his premises, and a member of the family should do likewise for those that are sent to the home. This is in order that in the days after the funeral acknowledgement may be sent to all those who have shown their sympathy in this way. No particular form of words is prescribed for cards accompanying gifts of flowers. Such phrases as:— "In affectionate memory," "With deep sympathy," and "In memory of a very dear friend," suggest themselves, but the exact wording largely depends on how well the sender knew the dead person, or on how friendly he is with his relatives.

Mourning

If it is particularly requested that there should be "No Mourning" this wish should be respected by friends who attend the funeral. They should, nevertheless, wear clothes of a sombre rather than of a bright colour. When the absence of any request to the contrary implies that mourning is to be worn, it is no longer essential that friends, as opposed to near relations, should be dressed in black. Men who go in morning coats will, of course, wear black waistcoats, black ties and black, not grey, top hats. If they go in lounge suits these, if not black, should be dark and, in any case, the tie should be black. Ladies who have black dresses should wear them, failing which they should appear in some dark or subdued colour. The near relatives will probably wear deep black.

Precedence at a Funeral

Friends attending a funeral should go straight into the church and take their places, a few pews in the front being reserved for the members of the bereaved family.

If the hearse containing the coffin is driven to the church from a mortuary or chapel attached to the undertaker's premises rather than from the family home, the undertaker will see to it that the hearse arrives before the cars bringing the family mourners. The choir and the officiating clergy will be waiting by the West Door of the Church to lead the way in front of the coffin, the relations following behind it.

At the funeral of a child, the parents walk immediately behind the coffin, their other children behind them. When one of a married couple has died, the surviving husband or wife, accompanied by the oldest child, walks first. A childless widow would usually be accompanied at her husband's funeral by a brother. Grandparents, uncles and aunts, walk behind the nearest relations of the dead person, followed by any other more distant relatives.

Leaving the Church

At the end of the Service the family mourners will file out of the church behind the coffin in the order that they entered it. If the body is then to be interred at the municipal cemetery or cremated, only the family mourners will accompany it on this final journey, probably travelling in the cars which had brought them to the church.

The main body of the congregation should therefore remain in the church for a few moments or, if they do come out, stand aside until the funeral cortège has moved off. If the body is to be buried in the churchyard where the funeral service has been conducted, friends may wish to be present and to file past the grave afterwards. But they should keep their distance, so that the relatives may be near the coffin at the graveside, as they were in church.

Period of Mourning

A long period of mourning was at one time demanded. Only by degrees and at lengthy intervals, as in a protracted transformation scene, was the transition from black to light shades effected. Not until this process was complete was it thought proper for people who had suffered bereavement to resume their normal activities and to play their former part in the social round.

Convention in this respect, as in some others, is now far less rigid. The change is due in part to a belief that preoccupation with the trappings of bereavement is mawkish and morbid: in part to a recognition that a person's memory may be cherished without recourse to outward signs of grief: in part to the fact that in the modern world the claims of business or household duties are imperative; in short, that life must go on. For most people therefore it is only in the employment of leisure hours that there is much room for choice. It is unlikely that in the early stages of bereavement the members of a family will feel disposed to dine in restaurants, go to dinners or entertain their friends. This, rather than any particular code of behaviour, provides the best reason for them to stay at home and to live very quietly. When they feel able and ready to go out and about it would be unreasonable to criticize them for doing so.

Friends, for their part, will understand and respect their attitude. The most considerate action friends can take is to let it be known that they are ready to help in any way possible, and to leave it to the members of the bereaved family to invite their assistance, advice or confidence when and as they wish. Some people find relief in talking about their loss, while others prefer not to refer to it. Friends should take the appropriate cue and act accordingly.

CHAPTER XI

MISCELLANEOUS

Table Manners

(i) *Unobtrusive Eating.*—One cannot put food into one's mouth without first opening it. But once the food is there, the lips should, so far as is possible, be kept closed while the teeth are chewing and biting so that it can be swallowed. It is unpleasing to see people eating when their mouths are open or talking with their mouths full. It is equally wrong to drink before the food already in the mouth has been swallowed. Similarly if one has a slice of bread, a roll or a bun, it is incorrect to raise it to the mouth and take a bite out of it. Instead, a small piece should be cut off with a knife or broken off with the fingers and conveyed to the mouth. This may not be possible at picnics, but we are concerned here with meals served at a table.

(ii) *Eating Fruit.*—Some people maintain that the skin of an apple is nutritious. If you subscribe to this school of thought, the correct procedure is to lay the apple on the plate, cut it in half with a knife and then bisect each half. The resulting quarters can then be divided further and each piece carried to the mouth on a fork. On informal occasions a person desiring to remove the skin is permitted to do so with a fruit knife. If he enjoys (and who does not?) removing the skin in one unbroken piece, he should nevertheless refrain from advertising his prowess by holding the apple so far above the plate that a foot or so of skin dangles freely downwards. At a dinner party, however, it is better to cut an apple or pear into four, impale each quarter in turn on a fork, and peel it with a desert knife.

Stewed cherries are usually fairly soft and the stones can mostly be detached on the plate. Should this work of separation take place in the mouth, the spoon should

be raised sideways and the lips opened just enough to allow the stone to be deposited in the spoon. Cherry stones should be placed in a small heap and not arranged in a line round the rim of the plate (Our days of playing 'tinker, tailor,' etc. are unfortunately over). With raw cherries the stones must obviously be detached inside one's mouth, and the fingers raised to the lips to remove them unobtrusively. The same applies to grapes, though the process is almost bound to be somewhat messier. But we have a napkin, and perhaps a finger-bowl in which to rinse our fingers.

(iii) *Oysters.*—If you encounter oysters—the author

of this book has only a nodding acquaintance with them —the procedure is to hold the shell steady with the left hand, slide a fork under the oyster with the right hand, raise it to the lips and make one mouthful of it. Small slices of brown bread and butter are often served with oysters, together with pieces of lemon and cayenne pepper. Some people do not like oysters. At a private dinner therefore they can only leave them in front of them, because, as the first course, half a dozen oysters on a plate may be ready at each person's place as he sits down. At public dinners such refusal is simple, and it is not unknown for one's neighbour at table gratefully to accept the additional portion.

(iv) *Asparagus.*—The cautious method is to cut the heads from the stalks with a fork and use the fork to raise the mouthful to the lips. The enterprising method is to raise the piece of asparagus in the fingers (usually in the right hand) and place the tip in the mouth. This method has its dangers. It is wrong to put only the extreme tip of the asparagus in the mouth and then nibble down it until the tough part is reached. It is equally wrong to throw the head back in a carefree manner (like an uninhibited consumer of spaghetti) and lower the asparagus into the mouth. Unless one can avoid these excesses, it is better to play safe—which, indeed, most people do.

(v) *Savouries.*—Although both knife and fork will probably be provided, it is more correct to use only the fork, but if the toast proves refractory it is preferable to use the knife as well than to ply the fork with frenzied desperation.

(vi) *Soup.*—If soup spoons are sometimes uncomfortably large to get into the mouth it is because they are not meant to. The technique is to fill the spoon, not quite to the brim, raise it to the mouth with the side, not the tip, towards the lips, and then open the lips wide enough to allow the contents of the spoon to be tilted gently into the mouth. In this way soup can be imbibed silently and without loud sucking noises.

When there is not sufficient soup left in the plate to enable the spoon to be filled, the plate should be tilted a little with the left hand, away from and not towards the person drinking it.

(vii) *Finishing Simultaneously*.—A man should not begin to eat until the lady next to him has started. This presents no difficulty as ladies are served first. It is desirable that all those seated at table should finish their course at approximately the same time. This, too, can easily be done, provided that one person does not monopolise the conversation.

(viii) *Smoking between Courses*.—This habit is prevalent in the United States, but over here it is not considered polite to smoke until coffee is served at the end of the meal. For one thing non-smokers at the table find it disagreeable. For another, it vitiates the taste, and is uncomplimentary to the food and to the person who has cooked it.

(ix) *Using Make-up at Table*.—There is no harm in plying a powder-puff in public. But peering into a mirror and screwing up the lips the better to be able to apply lipstick is an unengaging habit. Extensive repairs to the make-up should be carried out in the cloak-room.

(x) *Using a Knife*.—Americans are experts at reducing the use of a knife to a minimum. In this country there is no objection to using a knife for dealing with meat or poultry. But for such things as fish or savoury it is more elegant to use a fork, held in the right hand, and so far as possible to do without a knife. Similarly with a sweet course which is rather solid than liquid, a fork should be used for choice rather than a spoon and fork.

(xi) *Which knife and fork do I use?*—At a dinner-party with five or six courses on the menu, it is not always easy to know what implement is intended for which course. One solution is to wait until one's neighbour has begun and to be guided by his choice. As a rule, the cutlery is arranged so that what is needed for the first course is placed furthest from the plate, so that one works inwards as the meal proceeds. In case any hostess should herself be in doubt how the places should be laid at table, the general practice is as follows:—

Furthest on the right is the soup spoon. Next on the right and left respectively come the fish knife and fork, next inwards the large knife and fork for the main meat course, then a knife and fork for the savoury, next a fruit knife and fork for dessert and, lastly, on the right a small knife for cutting bread. The spoon and fork for the sweet course are usually placed separately from the rest, parallel to, not at right angles to the edge of the table.

Speech

It is sometimes said that, whereas a Scottish accent or an Irish brogue is unexceptionable and may even prove an asset, a man who speaks with a 'provincial' accent is likely to be at a disadvantage when he faces a Selection Board gathered together to consider candidates seeking posts in certain professions. To what extent there is nowadays any ground for this assertion it is hard to say.

The question, in any case, is irrelevant so far as this book is concerned.

Anyone who listens to the radio is aware that the intonation and pronunciation of one speaker may be markedly different from another's and also from those of the announcer who introduces the programme. On such occasions one does not need to be an expert in phonetics like Professor Higgins in Shaw's *Pygmalion* to be able to tell that one speaker hails, let us say, from Wales, another from Yorkshire, a third from the West Country, while the fourth speaks what is sometimes known as 'Standard English.' One of these voices may strike one listener as more attractive than another, while someone else may have a different preference. But essentially one is as good as another. For everyone to speak exactly alike would be just as uninteresting as for everyone to be or to look alike. The fact that people in the South usually pronounce castle with a long 'a' while Northerners generally do so with the 'a' short does not mean that one is better than the other or that one is right and the other wrong. Such differences are regional and variety of this sort is welcome and colourful. A regional accent is not something to be ashamed of. What is wrong is to try to conform to 'Standard English' by speaking in an affected manner. A local accent is preferable to a 'refained' one. The latter is artificial as can readily be detected because in unguarded moments it is discarded and the 'local' accent appears undisguised.

Correcting Defects of Speech

The foregoing remarks should not be taken as implying that faulty pronunciation should not be put right. Whatever the intonation or accent may be, the wrongly dropped 'aitch' is a mistake, hence the importance of taking trouble with young people in their formative years to see that they do not get into slovenly habits of speech. Vowel sounds are important, and there is no denying the ugliness of 'oi' for 'i') or, say, of 'thenks' for 'thanks.' This is not to suggest that anyone who thinks his pronunciation defective should take exaggerated pains in speaking, or he will become self-conscious and adopt a mincing artificial form of utterance which is far less desirable than an honest provincial accent. But if one is aware of defects it is worth while to take some trouble to put them right by listening carefully to those who do speak well and without affectation.

Slang

Colloquial expressions are often vivid and arresting, but they should not be overworked. This applies particularly to slang phrases. The fighting services, for instance, employ a technical jargon of their own, some terms of which become current elsewhere. But it is tiresome to hear a civilian making frequent use of expressions which properly belong to the terminology of the R.A.F. To use them in other contexts is out of place and ostentatious. Moreover they soon become little more than hack phrases. Slang is ephemeral, and to employ expressions which have had their day points to a poverty of vocabulary and a lack of sense of fitness on the part of the speaker. Slang, therefore, should be used with discretion.

Phrases to Avoid

Just as fashion decrees that it is wrong for a man to wear a top hat with brown boots or for a woman to smoke cigars in public (though it is done in Denmark), so there are certain words and phrases which, for no readily ascertainable reason, are not regarded as correct usage. Such, for example, are 'serviette' for 'table napkin', 'commence' for 'begin', 'bathing costume' for 'bathing dress', 'gift' (usually) for 'present', 'cycle' for 'bicycle', 'will you take a seat' for 'please, sit down', 'pardon' for 'I am sorry' or 'I beg your pardon' and 'pleased to meet you' for 'how do you do'.

The words 'lady' and 'gentleman' present certain difficulties. It would be wrong, for instance, in a conversation among equals to refer to a third party as 'a lady friend of mine.' One should say rather 'A girl I know' or 'A woman I know'. But if a stranger approached you in the street to ask you the way and, being uncertain, you stopped a passer-by, it would be correct to say to him: "I wonder whether you can help this lady (this gentleman) who wants to know the quickest way to the railway station." Since your enquirer is a stranger, it is polite to give him or her a social rank higher than may be strictly due.

The importance of the foregoing points and others like them can be exaggerated. If a person's speech is unaffected and his manner natural and friendly, any small social errors of which he may be guilty will readily be overlooked by sensible people.

Pronunciation of Foreign Place-names

When abroad one naturally tries to give to names of places the same pronunciation as that used by the inhabitants of the country. There are some places, however, which are so well-known that when speaking of them in this country it would be affectation for an

Englishman to use the foreign pronunciation, e.g. to give the French pronunciation of Paris, Marseilles or Monte Carlo. It would be equally silly to speak of Firenze in this country when you mean Florence or of Milano instead of Milan.

But save when places have, like Paris, or Copenhagen, a recognised English pronunciation, it is perfectly proper for a person to use the foreign pronunciation of a foreign place-name when he has occasion to mention it in this country. Thus while it would be affected and pedantic to say: "We are going to Barthelona (meaning Barcelona)" it would be correct to say: "Next year we hope to spend our holiday on the 'Costa Brava'," but wrong and ignorant to distort it into, say, 'Coaster Braver'.

Pronunciation of Surnames

English spelling, as long-suffering foreigners know only too well, is an unreliable guide to pronunciation (e.g. cough, bough, rough). The pronunciation of certain surnames is sometimes puzzling even to people whose native language is English. It is not often that one has occasion to pronounce such names, so some of them for that reason lead to mistakes. The following list, which is by no means exhaustive, may therefore be useful for reference. In some instances the stressed syllable is shown:—

Spelling	*Pronunciation*
Abergavenny	Abergénny ('g' hard)
Beauchamp	Beecham
Belvoir	Beaver
Berkeley	Barclay
Bicester	Bister
Bouchier	Bowcher

Spelling	*Pronunciation*
Buchan	Bucken
Cholmondeley	Chumley
Cockbain	Cobáin
Colquhoun	Cohóon
Compton	Cumpton (usually)
Conyngham	Cunningham
Coutts	Coots
Cowper	Cooper
Dalziel	Deéal
Derby	Darby
Dumaresq	Dumérrick
Elgin	Elgin ('g' hard)
Glamis	Glarms
Gough	Goff
Hertford	Harford
Home	Hume (usually)
Hotham	Hutham (like the 'o' in brother)
Ker	Carr
Knollys	Noles
Lefevre	Lefever
Lemaistre	Lemayter
Leveson-Gower	Loosen-Gore
McLeod	McCloud
Mainwaring	Mannering
Marjoribanks	Márshbanks
Menzies	Mínges (usually)
Meux	Muse
Moncton	Munkton
Montgomery	Mungúmery
Mowbray	Mobrey
Pepys	Peeps
Pontefract	Pumfret

Spelling	Pronunciation
Pytchley	Pytchley (as in 'sty')
Tollemache	Tolmash
Tyrrwhitt	Tirritt
Vaughan	Vorn
Wemyss	Weems

Foreign Phrases used in English

It is affectation to use foreign phrases when an exact English equivalent exists. But there are a number of expressions which have been borrowed from other languages, particularly French or Latin, and are now used in English.

It is important that the proper meaning of such expressions should be understood if they are to be correctly used. Here are some of them:—

Alibi.—In Latin this means 'elsewhere'. A man accused of committing a crime may seek to establish his innocence by proving an alibi, that is by showing that he could not possibly be guilty because at the time the crime was committed he was not on the spot. That is the only correct use of the word. It is a common mistake to use 'alibi' with the meaning of 'excuse'.

Au Pair.—To stay *au pair* in someone's house usually means receiving free board and lodging, but no salary.

A propos.—This means 'to the point', 'relevant'. Hence Mrs. Malaprop in Sheridan's *The Rivals* who had such a masterly power of misusing words. The phrase is often used with the meaning of 'By the way, while we're on the subject' or 'that reminds me'.

Blasé.—Used to describe an experienced or worldly-wise person who has become bored, indifferent, incapable of enthusiasm.

Bona fide.—Literally 'in good faith'. Used with the meaning of 'genuine'—a bona-fide applicant (for a job).

Buffet.—A sideboard or a (station) refreshment room. A 'buffet' supper means a 'stand-up meal' with the fare laid out on side-tables.

Carte blanche.—Literally a blank sheet of paper. To give someone 'carte blanche' is to allow them an entirely free hand, to give them authority in dealing with a given problem or undertaking.

Débutante.—To make one's 'début' is to make one's first appearance, for example, on the stage. Hence used of girls who have left school and are launching out into society.

De trop.—Too much, too many. Hence to be 'de trop' is used of a third person who is present when the other two would very much prefer to be by themselves.

e.g.—Short for *exempli gratia* and meaning 'for (the sake of) example': it is not to be confused with i.e. (*id est*) which means 'that is' or 'namely'.

Entrée.—Apart from meaning an intermediate course at dinner, the phrase occasionally occurs as 'to have the entrée' and is applied to someone who has the privilege of admission to some exclusive circle, e.g. to Court, or to the Royal Enclosure at Ascot.

Entre nous.—'Between you and me', 'between ourselves'. But why not say 'confidentially'?

Fête.—Feast, festival: hence an entertainment especially out of doors, as in garden-fête.

Mardi gras.—Shrove Tuesday.

Nom de plume, nom de guerre.—Assumed name, pen-name.

Passé.—Past one's best, out-of-date.

Pièce de résistance.—The main course of a meal, the chief item in a concert or theatrical show.

P.p.c.—*Pour prendre congé.*—To take leave, bid farewell. Rarely used now. The initials written on a visiting card indicated that the caller was leaving the district and was paying a final call before doing so.

R.S.V.P.—*Répondez s'il vous plaît.*—Kindly answer (on invitation cards).

Sang-froid.—Coolness, self-possession.

Savoir faire.—Social poise, knowledge of the ways of society.

Tête-à-tête.—A private confidential interview.

Trousseau.—An outfit of clothes, particularly a bridal outfit.

Restaurant French

It is not the practice of all hotels and restaurants in this country to write their menus in French, but many of them do. It is done also at some public functions, and private hostesses occasionally prefer French to English for this purpose. At all events some knowledge of French cooking terms is useful, and a few of them are set down in the following list:—

English	*French*
Clear Soup	Consommé
Turtle Soup	La Tortue des Indes
Thick Soup	Purée, Potage
Tomato Soup	Soupe Purée de Tomates
Smoked Salmon	Saumon fumé

Fried (boiled) Sole	Soles frites (bouillies)
(Savoury) Omelette	Omelette aux fines herbes
(Mushroom) Omelette	Omelette aux champignons
Veal Cutlet	Cotelette de Veau
Lamb cutlet with peas	Cotelette d'agneau aux petits pois
Roast Turkey	Le dindonneau rôti
Pickled pork	Le petit salé
Strawberries and Cream	Fraises à la Crème
Strawberry ice	Glace aux Fraises

Any hostess wishing to have a menu written in French would do well, if in doubt about the correct form, to revert to English, or else consult someone at a hotel or restaurant who has the necessary experience.

Conversation

The most enjoyable conversations are those that arise spontaneously between intimate friends who happen to hit on a stimulating or congenial topic. On such occasions talk flows freely. It is when people do not know each other well or have only just been introduced that conversation may prove difficult. In such circumstances it is a safe rule to steer clear of politics and religion. These are subjects on which people are liable to hold decided opinions, and it is rash to embark upon them or to be assertive or dogmatic, for either people may be stung into a heated argument or else, in the interests of good manners they do not speak their minds and chafe under a sense of restraint. Either way offence may be given and the conversation will languish.

Some people have a real gift for conversation. They have a ready command of words, a gay wit and a fund of experience or ideas. We cannot all hope to match them.

But if we ourselves take an interest in affairs of general concern, in books and plays, we can find things to talk about and, under the stimulus of good company, the right words in which to express our ideas. A good conversationalist does not dominate or lay down the law. He should allow others to have their say. A good story is welcome, but a succession of anecdotes is likely

to become tedious. It is rude to interrupt, especially when an older person is talking. When a conversation shows signs of leading to vehement argument or where the topic appears to be distasteful to one of those present, a well-bred person will drop the subject or divert the talk into other channels. Sarcasm at the expense of someone who is shy or stupid is unforgivable. Mimicry likewise should be employed with discretion. Malicious gossip about mutual acquaintances is in bad taste and may cause untold distress. Conversation is a social pleasure and it is through the words we exchange that we get to know people. If we subsequently decide that we dislike them or that they bore us, future contacts can be reduced to the minimum required by civility. But until we have so decided conversation provides the chief means of improving an acquaintance. We do not want only to like people. We also want them to like us. Hence the need to talk pleasantly, to find subjects of common interest. A good talker knows how to listen to others as well as to interest them in what he has to say. It is not his business to exhibit his superior knowledge or, when engaged in friendly conversation, to score debating points.

A father once took his son with him when he went to call on an elderly man. When they had taken their leave of him the son, with the naïve intolerance of his seventeen years, observed: "What a rum old bird!" "Yes," rejoined his father mildly. "I wonder what he thought of you!"

It is by our manners and our conversation that people, when we first meet them, are likely to form their opinion of us.